APPLIED MEASUREMENT IN EDUCATION, 18(1), 1–9
Copyright © 2005, Lawrence Erlbaum Associates, Inc.

GUEST EDITOR'S INTRODUCTION

Adapting Testing Technology to Serve Accountability Aims: The Case of Vertically Moderated Standard Setting

This article introduces the focus and contents of a special issue of *Applied Measurement in Education* devoted to vertically moderated standard setting (VMSS). The article begins by presenting some history related to the nexus of policy initiatives and psychometric capabilities. The policy context that necessitated the development of VMSS is described; the challenges of setting standards across grades and subject areas are explored; and a definition of VMSS is provided. Finally, brief descriptions of the contents of this special issue are provided along with appropriate acknowledgments.

I think, in general, that psychometrics is most appropriately viewed as a service profession. If an opinion researcher wanted to obtain the most accurate estimates of the public's views on an issue, psychometricians could provide—and have developed—innovative methods for attacking the problems inherent in that task, including sampling strategies, question construction, format, and timing. When personality researchers want to study that ephemeral construct, psychometricians have aided that quest with the development of projective techniques, methods of scaling responses, and so on. When college personnel needed less biased, more accurate, more efficient ways of helping them make important admissions decisions, the multiple-choice item format, item construction techniques, and optical scanning equipment were developed or extended by psychometricians to serve that need.

Psychometrics functions—or should function—as a helping profession. Often, however, the reality of how testing specialists are viewed is quite different from how they function. As an example, I can point to one of the most misunderstood social scientific phenomena: measurement-driven instruction (MDI). Regrettably, many educators and others misapprehend that practice to mean that testing special-

Requests for reprints should be sent to Gregory J. Cizek, School of Education, CB3500, University of North Carolina at Chapel Hill, Chapel Hill, NC 27599-3500. E-mail: cizek@unc.edu

ists—that is, psychometricians—somehow impose their will regarding important educational outcomes via the tests they create. Even some psychometricians have expressed this view, which can be seen in Madaus's (1988) (mis)characterization of MDI as "psychometric imperialism" (p. 84).

In fact, the phenomenon of MDI is not the horrible creation of mad psychometric scientists, but represents the insight of pragmatic policymakers that measurement services and technology could be appropriated in their struggle to achieve political or social goals. I have previously described this phenomenon in the context of minimum-competency testing:

> Mandated high school graduation tests and the student competency testing movement in general seemed to dominate the educational policy debates of the 1970s, with measurement specialists often called, cajoled, or willingly inserting themselves into the debates. My hypothesis here is that the high-stakes pupil testing of the 1970s was made inevitable because of poor decision making—or at least perceived poor decision making—and the resulting search for alternatives... It was during the tumultuous 1970s that complaints of some business and industry leaders began to receive broad public currency: "We are getting high school graduates who have a diploma, but can't read or write!" (Cizek, 2001a, pp. 6–7)

Legislators, in an attempt to be responsive to their business and industry constituencies, faced a difficult dilemma. One route to having an impact on what happens in classrooms would have been to allocate resources to teacher training, curriculum revision, professional development, and personnel evaluation. For simplicity, I call this route the "slow option of uncertain result." Collective bargaining agreements, academic freedom traditions, and the massive, monolithic institution of public education all mitigated against selecting this option.

A second route was to mandate a test—not any particular process, pedagogy, or professional practice. All that was required was the comparatively modest investment in the designing of a test and consequences associated with passing or failing it for either teachers, students, or both. I call this route the "rapid option of almost certain result." Given the alternative routes, the avenue of choice was obvious. Testing specialists were enlisted to respond to the mandate to produce high-quality tests aligned with specified content frameworks at reasonable cost. The rest, of course, is history... and English language arts, and mathematics, and science.

THE CONTEXT OF NO CHILD LEFT BEHIND

All of the preceding professional and historical background is intended to provide some context for history repeating itself. As was the case with the minimum competency testing impulse witnessed in the 1970s, the issue is again, in essence, accountability in public education. Education, perhaps one of the few remaining professions lacking meaningful accountability mechanisms, is clearly struggling to incorporate the nearly universally lauded concept of accountability into a system and culture in which the concept is both novel and radically transformative. As stated elsewhere, no one would argue that current accountability systems, relying as they do almost exclusively on student achievement measures, have reached a mature state of development. On the contrary, today's accountability systems are embryonic endeavors. However, to many policymakers, the public, and some professionals, the very introduction of accountability systems—even just acknowledging that accountability is a good thing—was an important first step. The camel's nose—as in the case of the minimum competency testing initiatives of the 1970s—is again high-stakes achievement tests (see Cizek, 2001b).

Again, with the passage of the No Child Left Behind (NCLB) Act of 2001, testing specialists are being pressed into service to provide technically responsive and professionally defensible solutions to a legislative mandate focusing on accountability and school improvement. In this case, the mandate requires states to demonstrate that states, districts, schools, and specified groups of students are making adequate yearly progress related to identified subject area objectives (i.e., content standards) in the areas of English language arts, mathematics, and science across several grade levels (3 through 8, plus one high school year).

According to the law, a key purpose of the legislation is:

> To determine the success of children served under this part in meeting the State student academic achievement standards, and to provide information to teachers, parents, and students on the progress being made toward meeting the State student academic achievement standards described in section 6311(b)(1)(D)(ii) of this title. [NCLB Act, 2001, § 6312 (b)(1)(A)(I)]

As is well known, the legislation contains key language regarding progress. According to the Act

> "Adequate yearly progress" shall be defined by the State in a manner that: (i) applies the same high standards of academic achievement to all public elementary school and secondary school students in the State; (ii) is statistically valid and reliable; (iii) results in continuous and substantial academic improvement for all students; (iv) measures the progress of public elementary schools, secondary schools and local educational agencies and the State based primarily on the academic assessments described in paragraph (3); (v) includes separate measurable annual objectives for continuous and substantial improvement for each of the following: (I) The achievement of all public elementary school and secondary school students; (II) The achievement of: (aa) economically disadvantaged students; (bb) students from major racial and ethnic groups; [and other specified subgroups]. [NCLB Act, 2001, § 6311(b)(2)(C)]

As is perhaps equally well known, the specification and measurement of progress have introduced significant psychometric challenges. One of the most substantial of the challenges has been that of creating a coherent system of performance standards across grades and subjects that will make inferences about progress meaningful and as accurate as possible. Or, it is perhaps more accurate to say that there exists a system of interrelated challenges.

CHALLENGES OF CROSS-GRADE AND
CROSS-SUBJECT AREA STANDARDS

Psychometricians have developed sound methods for linking tests across grades within the comparatively friendly context of norm-referenced testing (NRT). NRTs have typically been created by commercial test publishers who can impose stringent controls over the content and the statistical characteristics of test forms. The inferences traditionally supportable based on NRT performance (i.e., relative status of students) were also amenable to cross-grade linkages because a within-grade NRT could be designed to span a comparatively broad, cross-grade range of knowledge and skills. In the context of NRTs, the technology to accomplish the linking of tests across grades (sometimes called *vertical equating* when the constructs measured are the same and other conditions are met) represents reasonably well-developed psychometrics.

In contrast, the relatively newer assessment type—standards-referenced testing (SRT)—requires tests built to statistical specifications that routinely call for comparatively narrower targets and content specifications that are also narrower and tightly matched to specific within-grade content standards that often do not have considerable across-grade overlap. The content standards on which SRTs are based can thus militate against the construction of traditional cross-grade scales; vertically linking SRTs requires strong assumptions about the equivalence of constructs being assessed at different levels. The less stringent form of equating appropriate for such situations (actually not equating at all) is sometimes referred to as vertical scaling or vertical linking.

A second issue has to do with the existence (empirically determined or theoretically assumed) of a continuous, developmental construct across grade levels. Reasonable arguments have been made for the existence of an underlying developmental construct in, say, mathematics; equally well-reasoned arguments have been proffered to support the position that grade-to-grade mathematics achievement differs not only in quantity but in the nature of the construct assessed. Even linking two different tests that are designed to measure the same variable and express their scores on the same scale is viewed as a difficult psychometric challenge (see, e.g., Cizek, Kenney, Kolen, Peters, & van der Linden, 1999; National Research Council, 1998).

Other very specific challenges center on the sheer number of performance levels that the NCLB Act (2001) requires. According to the act, two levels representing higher achievement (*proficient* and *advanced*) are required, as is a lower level (*basic*). This need for multiple levels is compounded by the requirement of performance standards on three different tests (reading, mathematics, and science) at seven grade levels (Grades 3 through 8, plus one secondary). Thus, if a state implemented only the minimal requirements of the NCLB Act, a total of $3 \times 3 \times 7 = 42$ cut scores would be needed to delineate the boundaries of 84 performance categories.

However, it is not simply the sheer number of performance standards required that makes cross-grade linkage a challenge. The fact that the tests span such a wide grade (i.e., developmental) range introduces another layer of complexity. It would be considerably less of a technical feat to link SRTs in such a way as to permit fairly confident statements about progress between two adjacent elementary grades. It is quite a different matter to construct a scale that permits accurate inferences about progress between, say, Grade 3 and the senior year of high school.

The need for so many performance standards to be established can also be contrasted with several realities: (a) the fact that different standard-setting methods may be required depending on the nature, format, and other characteristics of a test; (b) the research evidence in the field of standard setting that different standard-setting methods often produce different results; and (c) the finding that, even when the same method is used on a test by equivalent groups of participants, resulting cut scores can vary, sometimes a great deal. These realities mean that a system of cut scores across grades within one content area could vary in ways that would be illogical if, in fact, there existed a continuously developed ability being measured and if standard setters were consciously trying to maintain a consistent standard of performance across grade levels.

Further, the panels of educators who participate in standard setting are only one source of potential variability in performance standards across grade levels. It is almost certain that the panels of educators and others who participated in the development of the content standards for those grade levels would not have been instructed, intended, or even have been able to create content standards of equal difficulty across the grades. In fact, it is a reasonable hypothesis that even if a consistent standard-setting procedure were faithfully executed for each grade level, observed variation in recommended performance standards across grade levels would be more attributable to the content standards development process than to the standard setting.

The same realities are reflected in the problem of coherence of standards across subject areas. A system of cut scores within a grade level across different areas could also vary. For example, standard setters could recommend cut scores for proficient that would result in 80% of students being classified in that performance category in reading; 30% in mathematics, and 55% in science. Such a result would be illogical if, for example, there were no educational reason to suspect differential achievement in the subjects, if the content standards for the areas were of approximately equal difficulty, if instruction were equally allocated to the respective content standards, and again if standard setters were consciously trying to maintain a consistent standard of proficiency across the subjects. And, as noted previously, there is often no reason to assume that the panels of educators and others who developed the content standards for these three subject areas were necessarily focused on creating content standards that were of equivalent difficulty across subjects. Thus, in this example, it may well be that the relatively lower performance of students in mathematics compared to reading can in part be attributed to the fact that the mathematics content standards are much more challenging.

WHAT IS VERTICALLY MODERATED
STANDARD SETTING (VMSS)?

As should be evident, the challenges to creating meaningful systems of performance standards across grades and subject areas are many. And, put bluntly, the development of psychometric procedures for linking standards-referenced tests across grade levels is in its infancy. Nonetheless, the requirement to do so demands that measurement specialists respond with first-generation technology proposals to advance the important problems of how to measure, report, and monitor the educational growth of all students.

VMSS—also sometimes referred to as a process of vertical articulation of standards—is a developing concept in response to this need. Lissitz and Huynh (2003) formally introduced the concept of VMSS into the psychometric literature as a tool for responding to the requirements of the NCLB Act (2001) to monitor adequate yearly progress of students with respect to the NCLB performance standard categories of basic, proficient, and advanced. Lissitz and Huynh (2003) defined VMSS as

> A judgmental process and a statistical process that, when coupled, will enable each school to project these categories of student performance forward to predict whether each student is likely to attain the minimum, or proficient, standard for graduation, consistent with NCLB requirements.

Although introduced in the context of the NCLB Act (2001), the use of VMSS is not necessarily limited to that situation, and may be adaptable to use whenever it is desired to establish meaningful progressions of standards across levels or to enable reasonable predictions of student classifications over time when traditional vertical equating is not possible. Of course, it remains to be seen if VMSS will provide satisfactory solutions to the contexts to which it is being applied, and speculation about how adaptable VMSS will be to other contexts is, well, speculation.

To say that VMSS is a developing concept is, to some degree, understating the state of the affairs. VMSS is really in its infancy; contradictions and complications abound.

Although somewhat of a caricature, it is not too far off the mark to define VMSS more baldly as post hoc, subjective smoothing of performance standards to satisfy policy exigencies, that is, not really standard setting at all. The current state of the art in VMSS essentially requires some "metapanel" of standard setters to take a series of jagged individual standards set across, say, Grades 3 through 8 by independent grade-level committees and even out the peaks and valleys in that achievement trajectory. Even if the grist of the metapanel's mill (i.e., the original performance standards set by grade- and subject-level committees) was obtained via an accepted content-referenced procedure (e.g., Angoff, 1971; bookmark; Mitzel, Lewis, Patz, & Green, 2001), the difficulty in maintaining a content anchoring is obvious. It is not at all clear whether VMSS will prove to be truly compatible with the SRT paradigm and, from a theory-development perspective, that question is probably one of the most fundamental for future research to address.

Likewise, from a practical perspective, the current state of the art in VMSS is that there exist essentially no established, grounded, rationales for how to smooth those jagged trajectories. Assumptions must be made about growth patterns in achievement across grade levels, about equivalence in quality of instruction and opportunity to learn across all grades and subjects covered, and about level of difficulty of content standards across grades and subjects. Is an assumption of linear (or cubic, or quartic) trend appropriate? Given the aforementioned assumptions, is any functional assumption appropriate? In short, even the most modest research-based guidelines for helping VMSS participants to decide how to go about their task are not yet available. Clearly, as a line of inquiry for measurement specialists, VMSS research and development is a growth industry.

CONTENTS OF THIS ISSUE AND ACKNOWLEDGMENTS

The foregoing limitations notwithstanding, the articles in this special issue of *AME* represent the best efforts of psychometricians to respond to the challenges of expressing student progress in meaningful ways. Each article was originally presented as part of a session at the 2004 annual meeting of the National Council on Measurement in Education and subsequently at the annual Large Scale Assessment Conference of the Council of Chief State School Officers.

The first article, by Daniel Lewis and Carolyn Haug, provides background on the need for VMSS, and presents a strong argument for aligning policy aims and psychometric methods to achieve coherent systems of educational assessments in general, and corresponding performance standards, in particular. Lewis and Haug also describe the results of implementing an approach to achieving such alignment for a state-level writing assessment administered across Grades 4 through 10 in Colorado.

The second article, by Steve Ferrara, Eugene Johnson, and Lee Wen-Hung, also provides background on VMSS and discusses possible alternatives. Then, Ferrara et al. describe an operational VMSS procedure used to set performance standards on a state-level, primary-grades reading assessment, and they provide the results of a simulation designed to explore the classification consistency (accuracy) of pre-dictions of subsequent grade performance based on examinees' performance-level classifications in a current grade. The simulation compares combinations of three different types of growth models and four plausible growth rates.

The third article, by Bill Schafer, examines VMSS from the perspective of the sponsoring agency or authority responsible for conducting and applying stan-dard-setting procedures; in kindergarten through 12th-grade applications, this is typically a state department of education. Schafer proposes four institutional crite-ria—consistency with the state's policy goals, legal defensibility, generation of as-sets, and efficiency of resource use—and examines these in light of traditional psychometric criteria suggested for evaluating standard-setting endeavors.

The next article, by Chad Buckendahl, Huynh Huynh, Teri Siskind, and Joe Saunders, recounts the road to a system of vertically moderated standards across Grades 3 through 8 for a state-level science assessment program in South Carolina. This case study details the VMSS process from test design through eventual adoption of the recommended performance standards by the state board of education.

The fifth article, by Huynh and Christina Schneider, describes the situations for which VMSS is a viable alternative to vertical scaling or equating, recounts the de-cision by the National Assessment Governing Board to move away from vertical scaling for the National Assessment of Educational Progress, and suggests how VMSS can be used to assist in monitoring student progress and to yield defensible score interpretations.

The final article, by Huynh Huynh, Karen Barton, Patrick Meyer, Sameano Porchea, and Dorinda Gallant, provides an example of VMSS applied to the South Carolina student assessments in English language arts and mathematics across Grades 3 through 7. Huynh et al. also evaluate the predictive qualities of a system of vertically moderated performance standards using data from operational admin-istrations of the state assessments.

In closing this introduction, some acknowledgments of those who helped coor-dinate this special issue are in order. First, I thank each of the authors who worked under difficult deadlines to bring the fruits of their research into the professional literature as rapidly as possible. Each deserves recognition for aiding in the knowl-edge generation and public service traditions of the academy by bringing new ideas for adapting testing technology to meet the demands of evolving account-ability mandates. I also appreciate the confidence, advice, and support of Barbara

Plake, under whose editorship, *AME* continues its role as a premier outlet for disseminating high-quality, practical measurement research to the field.

Finally, as I considered the state assessment programs that served as the research sites for the studies reported here, I was struck by all of the effort and commitment that professional colleagues in those contexts expend to promote high-quality assessment. I join the authors of the articles in this special issue in expressing admiration, support, and encouragement for the exemplary testing programs, high-quality information about student achievement, and important data on the success of school improvement initiatives that are the fruits of their labors.

REFERENCES

Angoff, W. A. (1971). Scales, norms, and equivalent scores. In R. L. Thorndike (Ed.), *Educational measurement* (2nd ed., pp. 508–600). Washington, DC: American Council on Education.

Cizek, G. J. (2001a). Conjectures on the rise and call of standard setting: An introduction to context and practice. In G. J. Cizek (Ed.), *Setting performance standards: Concepts, methods, and perspectives* (pp. 3–18). Mahwah, NJ: Lawrence Erlbaum Associates, Inc.

Cizek, G. J. (2001b). More unintended consequences of high-stakes testing. *Educational Measurement: Issues and Practice, 20*(4), 19–27.

Cizek, G. J., Kenney, P. A., Kolen, M. J., Peters, C. & van der Linden, W. J. (1999). *An investigation of the feasibility of linking scores on the proposed Voluntary National Tests and the National Assessment of Educational Progress.* Washington, DC: National Assessment Governing Board.

Lissitz, R. W., & Huynh, H. (2003). Vertical equating for state assessments: Issues and solutions in determination of adequate yearly progress and school accountability. *Practical Assessment, Research & Evaluation, 8*(10). Retrieved August 5, 2004 from http://www.pareonline.net/getvn.asp?v=8&n=10

Madaus, G. F. (1988). The influence of testing on the curriculum. In L. N. Tanner (Ed.), *Critical issues in the curriculum: Eighty-seventh yearbook of the National Society for the Study of Education* (pp. 83–121). Chicago: University of Chicago Press.

Mitzel, H. C., Lewis, D. M., Patz, R. J., & Green, D. R. (2001). The Bookmark procedure: Psychological perspectives. In G. J. Cizek (Ed.), *Setting performance standards: Concepts, methods, and perspectives* (pp. 249–282). Mahwah, NJ: Lawrence Erlbaum Associates, Inc.

National Research Council. (1998). *Uncommon measures: Equivalence and linkage among educational tests.* Washington, DC: National Academy Press.

No Child Left Behind Act of 2001. Pub. L. 107–110, 20 U.S.C. § 6301 (2002).

Gregory J. Cizek
Guest Editor

APPLIED MEASUREMENT IN EDUCATION, *18*(1), 11–34

RESEARCH ARTICLES

Aligning Policy and Methodology to Achieve Consistent Across-Grade Performance Standards

Daniel M. Lewis
CTB/McGraw-Hill
Monterey, California

Carolyn A. Haug
Measured Progress
Broomfield, Colorado

In a coherent educational assessment system, the relation between the cut scores across the grades of a content area should reflect the goals of the educational system moderated by the state of the standards within that system. In this article, we discuss the need for consistent cut scores across the grades of a content area; we present and interpret several models of consistency; and we argue that the No Child Left Behind Act (2001) provides an opportunity to bring articulated, consistent standards to contiguous-grade testing programs. We propose an additional step in the standard-setting process—the identification of an across-grade alignment model for each content area—and provide a case study to demonstrate how a sponsoring agency can identify appropriate models of consistency. We describe a standard-setting design that integrates the across-grade alignment model into the judgment process and discuss the results of an operational standard setting that utilized this design. We close with an analysis of the processes used to determine the across-grade alignment models in Colorado and discuss how informed policy can foster progress toward meeting the goals represented by the cut scores.

The outcome of setting performance standards is a set of cut scores that operationalize a set of performance levels. Perhaps because of the simplicity of the

Requests for reprints should be sent to Daniel Lewis, CTB/McGraw-Hill, 20 Ryan Ranch Road, Monterey, CA 93940. E-mail: daniel_lewis@ctb.com

outcome—a set of raw or scale scores—standard setting is often treated as a discrete task with respect to other components of the educational system. However, cut scores are operational representations of the goals of an education system; the cut scores represent the thresholds of various levels of achievement. Typically, the *proficient* cut score represents the minimal goal for all students, the point at which a student is deemed to have met a standard. In a coherent educational assessment system, all components should work together to prepare the student to meet or exceed that cut score; each component suggests the cut score.

There is a constant tension between the proficient cut score in a given grade and content area, and other components of a balanced education system. In a well functioning system the knowledge, skills, and abilities represented by the performance standards (i.e., cut scores) are consistent with those specified by the content standards and curriculum frameworks and with those that are taught in the classroom. The proficient cut score must represent a balance between what students should know and be able to do under ideal circumstances, and that which students do know and can do under the circumstances that exist. The proficient cut score set on an assessment written in English must be comparable to the proficient cut score set on an other-language assessment in the same grade and content area if the assessments are intended to be comparable. The proficient cut score set under one standard-setting method typically varies with the proficient cut score set by another standard-setting method on the same assessment, waiting for an informed policy decision to reconcile the discrepancy. The proficient cut score has many relations, a wide circle of colleagues.

The proficient cut score set at one grade of a multigrade assessment program begs to be consistent with the message sent by the proficient cut scores at other grades within the same content area. However, this does not always occur. For example, Ensign, MacQuarrie, & Beck (2002) noted in a discussion of standards set for the Washington Assessment of Student Learning, "Differences between [the] reading standard at 7th grade and the reading standards at both 4th and 10th grade may be too great to be seen as reasonable" (p. 35).

Inconsistent standards, that is, those set at different grades of a content area with differences too great to be seen as reasonable, send different messages to different participants in the educational system. Students see a confused relation between the effort they put toward their studies and the results of those efforts when they bounce between performance levels, not as a result of their efforts, but because of inconsistent cut scores. Teachers who begin a school year with a proficient student may prescribe a program of instruction based on the assumption that the student is on track toward meeting the current grade's goals when it may be that the characterization of the student as proficient is based on a different operationalization of proficiency in one grade than in the next. Parents may question the validity of the testing program when students' performance level is a function of grade rather than their childrens' efforts and achievements. The public may question the schools and educational system in general when they see explicit signs of inconsistency. The public may have a difficult time understanding why there are sometimes great disparities in the success of their schools from grade to grade.

In summary, we assert that performance expectations must increase coherently across the grades of a content area within a contiguous grade assessment program. Under the traditional benchmark grade testing paradigm, this does not always occur, due to a lack of guiding policy and accepted methodology. Thus, some states may be reconsidering the efficacy of existing performance standards as they fulfill the federal mandates to test in contiguous grades. In this article, we argue that the No Child Left Behind (NCLB) Act (2001) provides an opportunity to modify existing cut scores in concert with the setting of those for newly administered assessments to bring articulated, consistent standards to contiguous-grade testing programs. We propose an additional step in the standard-setting process—the identification of an across-grade alignment model for each content area—and provide a case study to demonstrate how a sponsoring agency can identify appropriate models of consistency. We describe a standard-setting design that integrates the across-grade alignment model into the judgment process and discuss the results of an operational standard setting that utilized this design. We close with an analysis of the processes used to determine the across-grade alignment models in Colorado and discuss how informed policy can foster progress toward meeting the goals represented by the cut scores.

THE NCLB ACT OF 2001: AN OPPORTUNITY TO ALIGN ACROSS-GRADE PERFORMANCE STANDARDS

Prior to implementation of the NCLB Act (2001), most states tested at several benchmark grades; only a few states tested contiguously across all or most elementary and middle school grades (Olson, 2002). Under the benchmark grade testing paradigm, standard setting tended to be a grade by grade activity; a lack of guiding policy and accepted methodology yielded only moderately successful efforts to foster consistency across the grades (Lewis, 2001, 2002). It is important that cut scores relate rationally when set only at benchmark grades but it may be less obvious when they do not. When several years separate the grades, a number of factors can be assumed to result in different levels of achievement across the benchmark grades.

However, as Ensign et al. (2002) implied, one of those factors, may be that the performance standards were not set with a consistent level of rigor across the grades.

With the signing of the NCLB Act (2001), all states are required to test reading and mathematics in Grades 3 through 8 and at least once in high school by the 2005 to 2006 school year. NCLB also requires that science be tested at least once at each of the elementary, middle, and high school levels by the 2007 to 2008 school year.

NCLB specifies goals for adequate yearly progress (AYP) and for improvement resulting in all students reaching at least the proficient level by the 2013 to 2014 school year. States developing new tests to meet the requirements of NCLB will also have to set new cut scores.

Because the NCLB Act (2001) introduces new stakes associated with the performance levels, there is cause to set new cut scores even for grades for which cut scores already exist. That is, the stakes associated with assessment results must be well-considered and integrated in the series of activities culminating in the adoption of cut scores. Linn, Baker, & Betebenner (2002) noted in their commentary on the implications of NCLB that "although many states have established performance standards for their tests, the standards were set unaware that they would be used to determine AYP objectives or that substantial sanctions would be associated with failure to meet AYP targets" (p. 4). Lewis (2001) indicated that "the stakes associated with the performance levels must be clearly identified prior to a standard setting. The consequences of [a student] placing or not placing in a given performance level have a strong effect on standard-setting participants' judgments" (p. 8). Thus, a strong argument can be made that cut scores should be reviewed and possibly reset across Grades 3 through 8 in reading and math in all states as the NCLB Act is implemented. This is true even for those states whose testing program already meets the requirements of the NCLB Act, if those states set cut scores without consideration of the consequences associated with the NCLB Act.

Thus, we assert that the new accountability measures associated with the NCLB Act (2001) justify a review of existing cut scores in concert with the setting of cut scores for assessments administered in new grades. This provides state departments of education an opportunity to affirmatively foster a coherent educational system with respect to the articulation of performance levels. In the next section, we consider several models of how cut scores might rationally relate across the grades of a content area.

MODELS OF CUT SCORE CONSISTENCY

The proficient cut score in a given grade should relate appropriately to the proficient cut scores at the grades above and below (when these grades are also tested) to enhance and reinforce the goals for student achievement at each grade. For this article, we assume that the role of the cut scores within the accountability model and the consequences associated with students placing in the various performance levels are similar across the grades. We define the proficient cut score as the location on the scale where a student has minimally met the current goals of the educational program as measured by the assessment.

Qualitatively, consistent proficient cut scores across grades within a content area should represent the knowledge, skills, and abilities required in each grade

adopted alignment models within the judgment tasks that occur during the standard-setting process.

INTEGRATING THE ACROSS-GRADE ALIGNMENT MODEL AND THE STANDARD-SETTING DESIGN

A bookmark standard setting was designed to support the writing and mathematics across-grade alignment models while preserving the ability of participants' judgments to strongly impact the cut scores. However, several significant modifications to the bookmark procedure were introduced. First, the participants setting cut scores for each grade of a content area worked at different tables in the same room. Each table had teachers with experience on grade and at the grade above or grade below. This was intended to promote participants from the various grades working together to achieve a common goal. At the opening session, participants were informed of the constraints of the alignment models, presented with the rationale for consistent cut scores across grades, and given an account of the steps taken to arrive at each alignment model.

Second, participants were provided with the preliminary cut scores, described previously, prior to the first round of ratings. This provided a starting point, a frame of reference, and an explicit example of the general pattern of results that their recommendation was required to mirror. Although participants had access to the scale score associated with the preliminary cut scores, their primary frame of reference was content based—the set of grade-level CSAP test items expected to be mastered by students at the preliminary cut score were identified for the participant.

Third, data were provided that served as tools to help participants understand (a) the implications of the alignment models, (b) the preliminary bookmarks and the judgment task, and (c) how judgments made at one grade related to those made at other grades within the same content area. Tables 4 and 5 give examples of the data provided for writing and math, respectively. The highlighted scale scores, bookmark locations, and expected number correct values represent the preliminary cut scores. (The scale scores, bookmark locations, expected number of correct values, and preliminary cut scores are all modified from those used in the workshop.)

As shown in Table 4, the preliminary cut scores for writing conformed to the equipercentile model and are represented as a horizontal line along the 59th percentile, indicating that 41% of students would fall at or above proficient. The preliminary cut scores for math conformed to a quadratic model. As shown in Table 5, a rise from left to right in the cells identifying the preliminary cut scores reflects the decrease in the percentage of students at or above proficient with an increase in grade. The preliminary cut scores derived for math indicated that 51%, 45%, 37%,

TABLE 4
Percentile to Scale Score to Bookmark Location to Expected Number Correct Tables for Writing

% Above	% Below	Scale Score								Bookmark Location								Expected Number Correct							
		G3	G4	G5	G6	G7	G8	G9	G10	G3	G4	G5	G6	G7	G8	G9	G10	G3	G4	G5	G6	G7	G8	G9	G10
1	99	468	493	511	533	565	603	623	653	63	74	73	74	67	70	72	74	62	74	73	73	68	72	73	73
2	98	444	471	491	515	547	579	600	625	61	74	73	72	65	69	71	72	62	73	72	71	67	71	72	72
40	60	354	372	388	404	432	450	460	477	52	56	52	51	42	57	49	50	55	60	58	56	52	59	58	59
41	59	**353**	**371**	**386**	**402**	**430**	**448**	**458**	**475**	**52**	**56**	**50**	**50**	**42**	**56**	**49**	**50**	**55**	**60**	**58**	**55**	**52**	**59**	**58**	**58**
42	58	352	370	385	401	428	446	456	473	52	55	49	50	42	56	49	50	55	60	57	55	52	59	58	58
98	2	27	67	97	107	117	127	137	147	8	9	7	6	6	6	5	5	19	18	12	18	18	20	17	16
99	1	27	67	97	107	117	127	137	147	8	9	6	5	5	5	4	4	18	15	11	17	17	18	16	14

Note. Preliminary cutscores are bold. G = Grade.

APPLIED MEASUREMENT IN EDUCATION, *18*(1), 35–59

Vertically Articulated Performance Standards: Logic, Procedures, and Likely Classification Accuracy

Steve Ferrara, Eugene Johnson, and Wen-Hung (Lee) Chen

American Institutes for Research
Washington, DC

Psychometricians continue to develop and evaluate methods for linking test scores, both horizontally and vertically. This article describes a social moderation process for articulating (i.e., linking) performance standards across grade levels for an operational state assessment program. The researchers used generated data to evaluate the likely classification accuracy of a Grade 2 performance standard that is intended to identify whether students are on track to achieve the proficient performance standard in Grade 3. The researchers evaluated classification accuracy for three plausible growth models and four amounts of growth; accounted for the effects of measurement error in the two tests; and illustrated the advantages of considering accurate, inaccurate, and uncertain classifications. Finally, the researchers discuss the usefulness of the social moderation process for linking performance standards in situations where overlapping test designs may not be feasible.

Psychometricians have been searching for decades for statistical procedures to link tests developed from different specifications—that is, linking procedures that produce stable and validly interpretable results (e.g., Ercikan, 1997; Johnson, 1998; Johnson, Cohen, Chen, Jiang, & Zhang, 2003; Linn & Kiplinger, 1995; McLaughlin & Bandeira de Mello, 2003; National Research Council, 1998; Slinde & Linn, 1977). Most of this work has involved applying existing statistical equating or regression procedures to link test scores from tests at the same grade level. Some of it has addressed linking test scores vertically across grade levels and schooling levels (e.g., elementary to middle schools). Vertical scaling and linking of test scores has been most successful when test design and item selection within and across grade levels are managed carefully so that sufficient overlap of items in adjacent test levels enables stable links. Examples of successful overlapping de-

---

Requests for reprints should be sent to Steve Ferrara, American Institutes for Research, 1000 Thomas Jefferson Street, NW, Washington, DC 20007. E-mail: sferrara@air.org

signs include Kindergarten through Grade 12 (K–12) commercial norm-referenced tests and individual intelligence and achievement tests. In some K–12 educational assessment situations, sufficiently overlapped test designs are not feasible. For example, it may not be feasible to overlap items for an individually administered kindergarten assessment of emerging reading skills and a group administered vocabulary and reading comprehension assessment for Grade 1.

The advent of the No Child Left Behind (NCLB) Act (2001; see also http://www.ed.gov/nclb) requirements for tracking cohort growth and achievement gaps across grade levels has spurred new thinking. Some psychometricians have proposed and conducted socially moderated (i.e., judgmental) procedures to link test performance standards from two or more adjacent grade levels (e.g., Ferrara, 2003; Lissitz & Huynh, 2003). In this article we describe (a) arguments that favor judgmentally linked performance standards over statistically linked test scores for some situations, (b) a judgmental approach for vertical linking of performance standards that has been used in an operational statewide assessment program, and (c) estimates of classification accuracy for vertically moderated performance standards using generated data. We call this judgmental approach to linking *vertical articulation.*

BACKGROUND

Only since the early 1990s have distinctions among types of test score links (i.e., equating, projection, statistical moderation, and social moderation) been explicated fully (see Linn, 1993; Mislevy, 1992). These explications provide a conceptual framework that has enabled creative thinking about procedures for linking scores and standards from different tests from the same grade level (e.g., Johnson, 1998; Johnson, Cohen, Chen, Jiang, & Zhang, 2003), and from tests for adjacent grade levels based on overlapping design specifications. The American Institutes for Research works with a state assessment program and its advisory committees to design and develop an articulated assessment system for Grades Kindergarten through 8 (K–8). This assessment system is intended to meet the NCLB Act (2001) requirements for assessing status within grade and annual growth across grades, and to achieve state goals to improve student achievement starting at kindergarten and continuing through middle and high school. We refer to this K–8 assessment system as *articulated,* because within-grade content standards and performance standards specify *proficient* performance within the grade level; proficient performance at a grade level predicts that students are on track to achieve proficient performance at the next grade.

The key concept in the vertical articulation process for setting performance standards is setting a performance standard in one grade that predicts performance in the subsequent adjacent grade. Specifically, and using Grades 2 and 3 reading as an example, standard-setting panelists considered the question, "What level of reading performance must students demonstrate in grade 2 in order to be considered *on track* for achieving proficient performance at grade 3?" Panelists considered this question with knowledge of the location of the Grade 3 cut score projected onto the Grade 2 score scale. A critical question about vertically articulated standards is how accurately do they predict performance in subsequent grades?

A full study of classification accuracy would involve administering successive grade-appropriate versions of tests to a single cohort of students over a period of years, assuring consistent exposure to the content standards of each grade level, and calculating the accuracy of classification. This process would require several years: Students would be given the Grade 2 version of the test as second graders and would be classified. A year later, these same students, now in the third grade, would be given the Grade 3 version of the test. The classification accuracy measure would be the degree to which prediction based on second-grade classification on the second grade test matches the actual classification of the students on the third-grade test, when they were in third grade. Of course, we need to know now, not later, whether the vertically articulated performance standards are accurate predictors of future performance. To speed up the evaluation, we have estimated classification accuracy of vertically articulated standards using simulated data generated under various assumptions about the changes in performance of the student population from Grade 2 to Grade 3.

VERTICAL ARTICULATION PROCESS

Assessment Design

In this article we report on research that is part of our work with a state assessment program and its advisory committees to develop assessments in several content areas. The content area standards and assessments for Grades K–8 are articulated in two ways. First, content standards overlap. At the highest level, reading content standards (e.g., apply strategies to comprehend and interpret Literary, Informational, Technical, and Persuasive Text) are the same for Grades K–12. Some grade-specific reading benchmarks appear at both Grades 2 and 3 (e.g., establish a purpose for reading, make predictions, and draw conclusions from text). Second, content-area instruction in one grade builds on the previous grade's instruction, with the intention of preparing students to succeed in the subsequent grade. However, grade-level indicators of benchmarks and standards are grade specific, and Rasch scaling of items and examinees is conducted independently for Grades 2 and 3.

The Grade 2 reading diagnostic assessment contains 45 items. Approximately 25 are multiple-choice items; approximately 20 are open-ended (the exact numbers vary across forms). Point values for the rubrics for the open-ended items range from 0 to 4. Of the 45 total items, 24 are discrete and 21 are associated with three reading passages. The Grade 3 reading achievement test contains 36 items—29 multiple-choice, 4 short-response (scored 0–2), and 3 extended-response items (scored 0–4)—associated with four reading passages.

In this study, we worked with the Grade 2 reading diagnostic and Grade 3 reading achievement assessments. The state assessment program includes other diagnostic assessments below Grade 2 and other diagnostic and achievement assessments above Grade 3. The Grades 3 through 8 assessments are in line with NCLB Act (2001) requirements. The standard-setting procedures we describe here for reading in Grades 2 and 3 were applied for reading assessments in other grades and for several grades in writing and mathematics.

Vertical Articulation Concept

The process for articulating performance standards across grades rests on the vertically articulated content standards. The concept of vertically articulated performance standards rests on the target performance standards: the proficient standard on the Grade 3 reading achievement assessment and the on track standard on the Grade 2 diagnostic assessment. The goal is that all students will perform at the proficient standard or higher at Grade 3. The purpose of the diagnostic assessment is to identify second graders who, based on their performance on the Grade 2 diagnostic assessment, are on track in Grade 2 to achieve at the proficient level in Grade 3. Schools and teachers then would have information about (a) which students are expected to achieve at the proficient level on the Grade 3 assessment, assuming they continue on the current achievement trajectory; and (b) for which students to provide intense instructional support to change the current achievement trajectory and increase chances that they will reach the proficient level on the Grade 3 achievement assessment.

We considered two approaches prior to settling on vertical articulation: linear interpolation, and judgmental standard setting with quasi-vertical item response theory scaling. These procedures represented early thinking when the intention was to have proficient performance standards at each grade and a cut score above and below that standard. They also represent alternative conceptualizations of what it means to articulate performance standards across grade levels.

Linear interpolation.   Initially, we proposed using the bookmark method (Mitzel, Lewis, Patz, & Green, 2001) to set standards for Kindergarten and Grade 3, and then establishing cut scores for Grades 1 and 2 using linear interpolation. Linear interpolation requires an assumption that growth in achievement across grades follows a straight-line trajectory with equal amounts of growth in achievement from one grade to the next. The steps in that process would have involved: (a) identifying the percentile in the Kindergarten empirical theta distribution corresponding to the Kindergarten on track cut score; (b) identifying the percentile in the Grade 3 empirical theta distribution corresponding to the Grade 3 proficient cut score; (c) aligning the percentile scales for Kindergarten, Grades 1, 2, 3, and 4; (d) drawing a line across percentile scales from the Kindergarten percentile to the Grade 3 percentile; and (e) finding the percentiles in Grades 1 and 2 that intersect that line. This procedure is similar to that followed for the South Carolina Palmetto Achievement Challenge Tests (see Huynh, Meyer, & Barton, 2000). The state department of education and its technical advisory committee rejected this approach because of concerns about the validity of the assumption of linear growth in achievement.

Judgmental standard setting with quasi-vertical scale scores. We also proposed to set standards in each grade using the bookmark method and assigning recommended cut scores to fixed Rasch scale scores. This procedure would have placed all scores on the same apparent scale across grades as a convenience for reporting and interpretation, even though the individual grade scales would be completely independent of each other. The cross-grade metric would be set judgmentally. For example, the Grade 3 proficient cut score, determined in the bookmark process, would be fixed at 350. Similarly, the Grade 2 proficient cut score on the independent Grade 2 scale, also determined in the bookmark process, would be fixed at 250. The cut scores above and below proficient on the Grade 2 scale would have been fixed to 275 and 225, respectively, and would correspond to the proficient cut scores on the adjacent grades above and below Grade 2, as judged by the panelists in their evaluation of the adjacent standards. That is, using Grade 2 as an example, the score of 250 would correspond to the cut score selected by the panelists as identifying the level of attainment of a *just barely proficient* second grader. The 275 would correspond to the cut score on the Grade 2 test that panelists felt would be achieved by a second grader who was performing, on the second-grade test, at the third grade proficient level. The 225 would correspond to the score, again on the second-grade test, of a second- grade student who was performing just barely at the first grade proficient level. This procedure does not require assumptions about equal-interval growth, as the cut scores are set separately for each grade. However, because the scores are set separately for each grade, there is no guarantee that the various cuts would really be predictive of performance in the subsequent year. The state department of education and its technical advisory committee rejected this approach because of its conceptual complexity and concerns about the actual predictability across grades.

Standard setting and vertical articulation. Unlike so-called vertical equating, the vertical articulation process does not involve statistical linking of scores across grade levels. It relies on the judgments of content experts about item response requirements, the state reading content standards, and the performance-level descriptors used for reporting test performance and standard setting.

STEPS IN THE STANDARD SETTING
AND ARTICULATION PROCESS

A panel of 24 educators and community representatives was trained on the state's Grade 3 reading content standards, assessment design, and performance-level descriptors and on the bookmark process. Nineteen of the panelists were teachers, three were other educators (e.g., a principal), and two were community representatives. Panelists learned about and then practiced the bookmark process. Working in groups of four or five, they examined each item in the ordered item booklet and answered two questions for each item:

1. What does a third grader need to know and be able to do in order to respond successfully to this item?
2. What makes this item more difficult than the items that precede it in the ordered item booklet?

Answers to these questions were intended to prepare panelists to make the bookmark judgment for setting a cut score. Panelists were directed to "Place the bookmark on the page where you would expect two thirds of third grade students who are just barely proficient to respond successfully." They also learned an alternate interpretation of the judgmental task: "Place the bookmark on the page where third grade students who are just barely proficient would have a 67% chance of responding successfully." Panelists were trained to understand that students who are just barely proficient would have less than a 67% chance of responding successfully to the item on the subsequent page and a 67% chance or higher on the previous items. In Rounds 2 and 3 of the standard-setting process, panelists received feedback on (a) pages on which other panelists placed their bookmarks (referred to as "agreement" information) and (b) percentages of students who would have reached the proficient level (referred to as "impact" information). Panelists followed discussion procedures and used focus questions to assure that they examined and considered all feedback systematically. They were directed to consider the feedback information to clarify their thinking about item response requirements and difficulty and to reconsider the appropriateness of the location of their bookmark in the ordered-item booklet. After completing three rounds to establish the proficient cut score, panelists followed similar procedures to establish an *advanced* cut score above the proficient cut score and a *basic* cut score below, resulting in four performance levels for Grade 3 reading. In all cases, the final cut score was determined as the theta score corresponding to the median page number, where the median page number was calculated across all panelists.

A second panel convened to establish on track cut scores for Kindergarten and each of Grades 1 and 2. This panel of 24 included 19 teachers from Grades K–3, 3 other educators (e.g., a local superintendent), 1 professor of reading, and 1 parent. They participated in training and practice, as described previously, and beginning with the Grade 2 diagnostic assessment, examined the ordered-item booklet and answered the two questions described previously. Their training included specific focus on creating articulated performance standards, the articulated design of the state reading-content standards, and the procedures they would follow to articulate performance standards across grades. In Round 1, panelists placed their book-marks in the ordered-item booklet in response to the direction, "Place the book-mark on the page where you would expect two thirds of third-grade students who are just barely on track to respond successfully." In Round 2, they received and discussed agreement information and impact information, which they discussed systematically in the same way as the first panel.

Then panelists received articulation feedback information and began the process of articulating the Grade 2 on track standard with the Grade 2 proficient standard. At this point, a representative group of five members of the Grade 3 standard-setting panel participated with the K–2 panel in discussion of articulation feedback information. The articulation feedback information identified the page in the Grade 2 ordered-item booklet that corresponded to the same percentile score in the Grade 2 scale score distribution as the percentile score in the Grade 3 distribution that corresponded to the Grade 3 proficient cut score. Panelists were instructed to consider the item and item response requirements on (a) this page, (b) the page on which their individual bookmarks were currently located, and (c) the pages in between. They were instructed to consider whether they should change their judgments about item response requirements and placement of the bookmark in light of this new information. Specifically, panelists considered whether students who are just barely on track should be expected to respond successfully to any or all of the items between their current Grade 2 bookmarked page and the projected Grade 3 page, and whether 67% of those students who are just barely on track should be expected to respond successfully to an item in that sequence of pages. In Round 3, panelists again considered agreement, impact, and articulation feedback.

Panelists followed the same procedures to articulate on track performance standards for Grade 2, Grade 1, and Kindergarten. Other standard-setting panels followed similar procedures to establish vertically articulated standards in two other content areas. In all cases, the final cut score was determined as the theta score corresponding to the median page number, where the median page number was calculated across all panelists.

RESULTS OF VERTICALLY ARTICULATING STANDARDS

The standard-setting panels recommended final cut scores on the theta scale of 1.27 in Grade 2 and 0.88 in Grade 3. The K–2 standard-setting panel intentionally set the Grade 2 cut score higher (in the Grade 2 theta metric) than the Grade 3 cut score (in the Grade 3 metric). These panelists made clear in discussion that they were more concerned about Grade 2 students who need remediation not receiving that remediation, and less concerned about some Grade 3 students who reached on track in Grade 2 receiving remediation unnecessarily. In these discussions they were referring in everyday terms to false negative errors (in the first case) and false positive errors (in the second case).

We present final recommended cut scores (i.e., page numbers in the ordered item booklet) for the Grade 3 reading proficient level and the Grade 2 on track level in Table 1. We also have included impact and articulation information for Grades K–2.

As is evident in Table 1, the page number that corresponds to the final recommended cut scores corresponds closely to the articulation page number for Grades 2 and 1. Likewise, the percentages of all students who would have achieved the on-track level in Grades 2 and 1 are similar to the percentage reaching proficient in Grade 3. The page number that corresponds to the final recommended cut score for Kindergarten is higher than the articulation page number. The percentage of all students reaching the on track level is lower in Kindergarten than in the other grades.

Table 2 provides information on the influence of the three types of feedback—agreement, impact, and articulation—on bookmark placements in Round 2 of standard setting. As the table indicates, the overall median bookmarked page did not change as a result of discussion at the beginning of Round 2 of the feedback information from Round 1. However, feedback and discussion appears to have influenced individual panelist bookmarked pages. In Round 2, tables and individual panelists with bookmark placements earliest in the ordered-item booklet moved their bookmarks closer to the table and panel median page numbers. Because the three types of feedback were presented at the beginning of Round 2, it is not possible to distinguish the influence of articulation information on bookmark placement decisions in Round 2. Panelist responses to the workshop evaluation form provide some insight. Of the 19 K–2 panelists who completed an evaluation form,

- 12 strongly agreed that the articulation information gave them information they needed to complete their assignment; 6 agreed with the statement, and 1 disagreed.
- 10 strongly agreed with the statement that the articulation information was very important in their placement of the bookmark; 7 agreed that it was somewhat important; 2 agreed that it was not important.
- In comparison, 11 strongly agreed with the statement that the agreement information was very important in their placement of the bookmark; 7 agreed that it was somewhat important, and 1 agreed that it was not important.
- Also in comparison, 8 strongly agreed with the statement that the impact information was very important in their placement of the bookmark; 9 agreed that it was somewhat important, and 2 agreed that it was not important.

Of the 18 responding panelists, 16 reported general satisfaction with the placements of the three on track cut scores. One panelist would have moved the Kindergarten bookmark one page lower. One panelist would have moved the Grade 2

TABLE 1

Grade 3 Proficient Cut Score and On Track Cut Scores for Grades K–2 and Accompanying Feedback

Variable	Page Number	Percentage Raw Score	Impact						
			All Students	Girls	Boys	White	Black	Hispanic	Multiracial
Grade 3 proficient cut score	24	61	72	76	70	78	48	59	67
Grade 2 articulation information	45	—[a]	72	75	69	77	51	61	67
Grade 2 on track cut score	45	75	72	76	69	77	51	62	67
Grade 1 articulation information	48	—[a]	70	73	66	73	53	55	70
Grade 1 on track cut score	47	73	77	80	75	80	64	66	77
Kindergarten articulation information	49	—[a]	77	81	74	79	67	67	72
Kindergarten on track cut score	54	82	68	72	64	70	56	59	61

Note. Maximum possible score and last page number is 49 in Grade 3, 65 in Grade 2, 62 in Grade 1, and 65 in Kindergarten. Impact is the percentage of students in each group achieving the proficient or on track level. K = Kindergarten.

[a]Panelists did not receive this information.

TABLE 2
Influence of Feedback Information on Bookmarked
Page Numbers in Round 2

Variable	Panel Median	5 Panelist Tables		24 Panelists	
		Lowest	Highest	Lowest	Highest
Grade 2					
Round 1	45	43	49	40	49
Round 2	45	44	48	43	49
Grade 1					
Round 1	47	44	55	43	56
Round 2	47	47	55	46	55
Kindergarten					
Round 1	52	46	58	41	58
Round 2	52	51	56	50	58

bookmark two pages higher; 4 would have moved the Grade 1 bookmark an average of over 6 pages higher.

Discussions among panelists at the beginning of Rounds 2 and 3 during standard setting for Grades K–2 tended to focus on two general topical areas: (a) whether all students and on track students at each grade could be expected to have learned the knowledge and skills required by the test items, and (b) setting fair performance standards. Panelists regularly referred to setting performance standards that are fair to students. They discussed fairness in two ways: setting on track cut scores that would identify (a) students in each grade who clearly would need the intensive intervention that would ensue by not reaching the on track cut score, and (b) percentages of students for whom the range of school systems in this state could be expected to provide intensive intervention. Panelists also discussed, in everyday-logic terms, notions of weighing false positive and false negative rates against one another.

Standard-setting panelists, the state department of education, and its advisory committees seemed satisfied with the recommended cut scores, impact information, and standard-setting process. The State Board of Education adopted the cut scores as recommended. Panelists' comments suggested that they also were aware that the on track performance standards may or may not prove to be accurate predictors of reaching on track and proficient levels.

A full study of classification accuracy would involve administering successive grade-appropriate versions of tests to a single cohort of students over a period of years and calculating the accuracy of classification. Of course, the state department of education needed to know immediately—not later—whether the vertically articulated performance standards would be accurate predictors of future performance. In addition, as one or two panelists observed early in training, the goal is to intervene with students to assure that more and more students each year would reach the on track level in Grades K–2 and that students who failed to reach on track in a grade would reach on track or proficient in the subsequent grade. Thus, instructional interventions would undermine accurate estimation of the classification accuracy of the on track standards. To address the state's need, we generated data to evaluate the accuracy of the Grade 2 on track cut score for predicting Grade 3 reading proficient performance. We describe the process of simulating data and discuss classification accuracy results in the next section of this article.

SIMULATION OF ACHIEVEMENT GROWTH AND CLASSIFICATION ACCURACY RESULTS

To evaluate the likely classification accuracy of the Grade 2 on track cut score, we generated data for three types of growth (i.e., growth models) and four amounts of growth. We estimated hypothetical distributions of Grade 3 reading proficiency under the following models:

- Linear growth model, in which the proficiency of all examinees increases by a fixed amount. Examinee positions in the distribution do not change relative to one another. This model serves as a benchmark for considering results from the other two growth models.
- Remediation model, in which the proficiency of examinees below the on-track level at Grade 2 increases at Grade 3 more than the proficiency of other examinees. This model reflects the possible outcome of intense remediation in reading during Grade 3 for all students who did not reach the on track level in Grade 2, that is, more rapid growth toward the Grade 3 proficient level than for other students.
- "Rich get richer" model,[1] in which the proficiency of examinees above the on track level at Grade 2 increases at Grade 3 more than the proficiency of other examinees. This model reflects the possible outcome of no or ineffective remediation in reading during Grade 3 for students who did not reach the on-track level in Grade 2: Reading proficiency would increase more rapidly for students above the on track level in Grade 2 than for students who were below the on track level in Grade 2.

In addition, we examined four amounts of growth:

- Negative growth. All Grade 3 thetas were set .39 units lower than the empirical Grade 2 thetas. This amount of growth covers the distance between the Grade 2 on track cut score (i.e., 1.27 on the Grade 2 theta scale) and the Grade

---

[1]We chose this label to describe the well known observation that the achievement of high achievers, as measured on educational tests, tends to grow at a faster rate than the achievement growth of low achievers.

3 proficient score (i.e., .88 on the Grade 3 theta scale). In this situation, the percentages of students achieving on track at Grade 2 and proficient in Grade 3 are equal.

* No growth. All Grade 3 thetas were set equal to the original Grade 2 thetas. In this situation, the percentage of students reaching proficient in Grade 3 is higher than the percentage that reached on track in Grade 2. This is because the Grade 3 cut score is lower in the Grade 3 theta scale than is the Grade 2 cut score in the Grade 2 theta scale.
* Low growth. All Grade 3 thetas were set .39 units higher than the original Grade 2 thetas.
* Moderate growth. All Grade 3 thetas were set .78 units higher than the original Grade 2 thetas.

Finally, we also accounted for the measurement error in the Grade 2 and Grade 3 assessments. We classified students into three groups in each grade: *clearly on track* (in Grade 2) or *clearly proficient* (in Grade 3), *clearly not on track* (in Grade 2) or *clearly not proficient* (in Grade 3), and *uncertain*. We created the uncertain classification by estimating 95% confidence intervals around each cut score using the Rasch model ability estimate standard error corresponding to each cut score and classifying as uncertain all examinees whose Grade 2 or Grade 3 score fell within the confidence interval.

Procedures

We simulated the Grade 3 results for the three growth models and four growth amounts using linear transformations of the empirical Grade 2 frequency distribution. We started with the empirical distribution of Grade 2 proficiency estimates (i.e., the theta estimates from the Grade 2 reading test) and estimated from that observed proficiency distribution hypothetical Grade 3 proficiency distribution estimates for the same population of students for the 12 conditions (i.e., four amounts of growth crossed with three growth models). We estimated individual proficiencies using:

$$\theta_3 = \theta_2 + [\alpha + \beta \times f(\theta_2)]$$

where θ_3 = the proficiency estimate at Grade 3, θ_2 = the proficiency estimate at Grade 2, and α, β, and $f(\theta_2)$ are defined as follows.

The parameter α has four conditions defined as the four amount-of-growth conditions described previously. The parameter β was set to .25.[2] The function $f(\theta_2)$

---

[2]This parameter specifies a slope for the growth curves for the three growth types. A slope of .25 reflects the modest increase in achievement test score variance that typically occurs across elementary school grades and is referred to as the "fan spread effect." Sensitivity testing for a more severe slope, 1.0, indicates influences on results, but only for the remediation growth model. The influence is a reduction in uncertainty rates, which occurs because the more severe slope moves the bottom of the growth curve to the right; a reduction in hit rates and an increase in false positive rates is displayed in Table 6.

has three conditions corresponding to the conceptual growth models described earlier. They are:

$f(\theta_2) = 0$, which is the linear growth model;

$f(\theta_2) = (\theta_c - \theta_2)_+$, which is the remediation growth model.

$f(\theta_2) = f(\theta_2 - \theta_c)_+$, which is the rich get richer growth model.

In conditions 2 and 3, the subscript "+" indicates that the value of the quantity in the parentheses is returned if the quantity is positive, while a value of 0 is returned if the quantity is negative. The function $f(\theta_2)$ has the effect of compressing the bottom and stretching the top of the simulated Grade 3 distributions for the remediation and rich get richer models, respectively.

Classification accuracy and accounting for measurement error in the Grades 2 and 3 assessments.   We examined likely classification accuracy in two ways. First, we examined results for the three growth models and four growth conditions, disregarding measurement error in the Grade 2 and Grade 3 test scores and the effects of those measurement errors on classification accuracy in Grade 3. Second, we accounted for the effects on classification accuracy of the measurement error in the Grade 2 and Grade 3 assessments. We estimated 95% confidence intervals around the Grade 2 and 3 cut scores using the Rasch model ability standard error at each cut score. Then we classified examinees in Grade 2 as clearly on track, clearly not on track, or uncertain. Similarly, we classified examinees in Grade 3 as clearly proficient, clearly not proficient, or uncertain for the three growth models and four growth amounts. These classifications produce nine possible classification outcomes for examinees, as portrayed in Figure 1.

To summarize classification accuracy, we first calculated the total numbers and percentages of examinees in the uncertain outcomes, separately for Grades 2 and 3. In Figure 1, these are outcomes 2, 4, 5, 6, and 8. Setting aside these examinees, we then calculated the true positive classification rate (i.e., clearly on track and clearly proficient in Grades 2 and 3, Outcome 1 in Figure 1), true negative classification rate (i.e., below the cut score in both grades, Outcome 9), false positive classification rate (i.e., above the cut score in Grade 2, below the cut score in Grade 3, Outcome 3), and the false negative classification rate (i.e., below the cut score in Grade 2, above the cut score in Grade 3, Outcome 7). We estimated coefficient kappa (e.g., Berk, 1984), which can be interpreted as a test's contribution to classification consistency, taking into account consistency due to chance.

Results

In this section, we describe simulation results prior to accounting for the effects of measurement error on classification accuracy. We describe classification accuracy results both before and after accounting for measurement error.

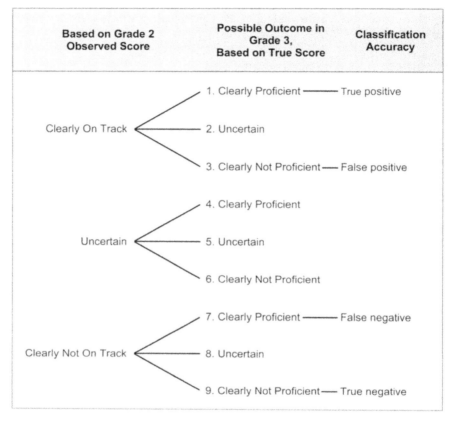

Based on Grade 2 Observed Score	Possible Outcome in Grade 3, Based on True Score	Classification Accuracy

FIGURE 1   Possible classification outcomes when measurement error is accounted for in the Grade 2 and Grade 3 assessments.

Simulated theta distributions.   Table 3 contains the descriptive statistics for the 12 type by amount growth conditions. The means and standard deviations in Table 3 are as expected: Negative-growth means were lower than no-growth means; low- and moderate-growth means were higher than no-growth means; standard deviations for the Grade 2 empirical data and the linear- and remediation-growth means remain unchanged; the standard deviations and skewness for the remediation growth model were smaller in comparison due to the shift to the right in the left side of the distribution that is introduced by that growth model; and the standard deviations for the rich get richer growth model were highest of all, due to the shift to the right in the right side of the distribution that is introduced by that growth model. (The Grade 2 empirical mean and standard deviation are not equal to {0, 1} as might be expected; they are the mean and standard deviation for the

TABLE 3
Descriptive Statistics for the Grade 2 Empirical Data
and 12 Sets of Simulated Grade 3 Data

Growth Amount	M	SD	Max	Min	Skewness	Kurtosis
Grade 2 empirical data						
Grade 2 empirical	1.77	1.11	6.42	−3.79	−0.34	1.13
Linear growth model						
Negative	1.38	1.11	6.03	−4.18	−0.34	1.13
No	1.77	1.11	6.42	−3.79	−0.34	1.13
Low	2.16	1.11	6.81	−3.40	−0.34	1.13
Moderate	2.55	1.11	7.20	−3.01	−0.34	1.13
Remediation growth model						
Negative	1.44	1.01	6.03	−2.92	0.05	0.75
No	1.83	1.01	6.42	−2.53	0.05	0.75
Low	2.22	1.01	6.81	−2.14	0.05	0.75
Moderate	2.61	1.01	7.20	−1.75	0.05	0.75
Rich get richer growth model						
Negative	1.57	1.29	7.31	−4.18	−.03	0.81
No	1.96	1.29	7.70	−3.79	−.03	0.81
Low	2.35	1.29	8.09	−3.40	−.03	0.81
Moderate	2.74	1.29	8.48	−3.01	−.03	0.81

Note. $N = 9{,}933$ in all statistics. Max = maximum; Min = minimum.

items selected from the entire item pool and included in the ordered-item booklet used for standard setting.)

Line graphs representing each of the growth types by amount models appear in Figures 2 through 4. As with the descriptive statistics, the shapes and locations of these distributions are as expected. Although the effects of the remediation growth model on the shapes of the line graphs in Figure 3 may not be readily apparent to the eye, the effects of the rich get richer growth model are apparent in Figure 4. For example, the low-growth and moderate-growth curves each display a "bump-out" to the right at $\theta = 2.16$ (i.e., the distribution mean of 1.77 plus .39 growth amount) and 2.55 (i.e., the distribution mean of 1.77 plus .78 growth amount) respectively, corresponding to the change in growth trajectories for those models.

Simulated Grade 3 performance results.   Table 4 displays the projected percentages of third graders who would reach the proficient level on the Grade 3 reading assessment, based on applying the Grade 3 cut score ($\theta = 0.88$) to the theta distributions estimated under the 12 growth model conditions. Measurement error is not accounted for in the results in Table 4.

As expected in this simulation, percentages of examinees reaching the proficient level increase in Table 4 as the amount of growth increases. Results for the linear and rich get richer growth models were the same. This is because the rich

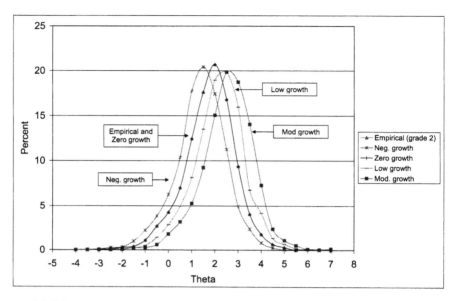

FIGURE 2   Distributions of empirical (Grade 2) and simulated (Grade 3) thetas for the linear growth model with four growth amounts.

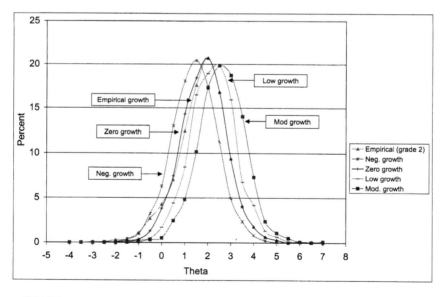

FIGURE 3   Distributions of empirical (Grade 2) and simulated (Grade 3) thetas for the remediation growth model with four growth amounts.

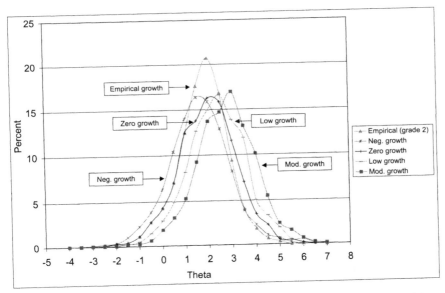

FIGURE 4   Distributions of empirical (Grade 2) and simulated (Grade 3) thetas for the rich get richer growth model with four growth amounts.

get richer model is the linear model stretched out on its right side, above the Grade 3 cut score.

Classification accuracy results.   Agreements between (a) empirical classifications of Grade 2 examinees below and at/above the on track level, and (b) projected classifications of the same examinees below and at/above proficient on the Grade 3 assessment appear in Table 5. Table 5 contains percentages of hits (i.e.,

TABLE 4
Percentages of Examinees Who Would Reach the Proficient Level in Grade 3 for Three Hypothetical Growth Models

Growth Amount	%
Linear and rich get richer growth models	
Negative	70.8
No	81.1
Low	87.5
Moderate	92.1
Remediation growth model	
Negative	70.8
No	83.6
Low	90.8
Moderate	95.1

TABLE 5
Classification Accuracy of Grade 2 On Track Standard
for 12 Hypothetical Grade 3 Scenarios

		Classification Errors		
Growth Amount	Hits	False Negative	False Positive	κ
Linear growth model				
Negative	100.0	0.0	0.0	—
No	89.7	10.3	0.0	.72
Low	83.3	16.7	0.0	.51
Moderate	78.7	21.3	0.0	.34
Remediation growth model				
Negative	100.0	0.0	0.0	—
No	87.3	12.7	0.0	.65
Low	80.0	20.0	0.0	.40
Moderate	75.7	24.3	0.0	.22
Rich get richer growth model				
Negative	100.0	0.0	0.0	—
No	89.7	10.3	0.0	.72
Low	83.3	16.7	0.0	.51
Moderate	78.7	21.3	0.0	.34

Note. κ = kappa coefficient; all other entries are percentages.

correct classifications above or below the cut score on both tests), false positive errors (i.e., students on track on the Grade 2 assessment and below proficient on the Grade 3 assessment), and false negative errors (i.e., students not on track on the Grade 2 assessment who reached proficient on the Grade 3 assessment). As before, measurement error is not accounted for in the results in Table 5.

Table 5 contains several interesting results.[3] First, there were no false positive errors for any growth type by amount model. This occurs because the Grade 2 cut score was high within the Grade 2 theta scale (i.e., 1.27) relative to the location of the Grade 3 cut score in the Grade 3 theta scale (i.e., 0.88). This result is consistent with panelist discussions about fairness of the cut scores, as described previously. In addition, the results for the linear and rich get richer growth models were the same. Because the Grade 2 cut score was higher in its distribution relative to the Grade 3 cut score in its distribution, under the linear model, all students who reach on track in Grade 2 will reach proficient in Grade 3. The same holds for the rich get richer model. On its left side, the rich get richer model is equivalent to the linear model; on its right side, it is stretched out, beginning at each of the growth amount starting points, all of which are at or above the Grade 3 cut score. Also, the hit rates

---

[3]We do not discuss the negative growth scenario in this section because the Grade 3 cut score was selected to assure 100% hit rates.

under these 12 hypothetical scenarios appeared fairly high, at least for the no-growth amount. This result occurs because the K–2 standard-setting panel set the Grade 2 performance standard low enough on the Grade 2 test difficulty scale (i.e., and the Grade 2 reading proficiency distribution) to avoid false negative errors and high enough so that the hit rate was near 90% for all three growth models. This result is also consistent with panelist discussions about fairness of the cut scores. Specifically, the true positive classification rate for all 12 scenarios is 70.8%. The true negative classifications in these data range from a low of 4.9% for the moderate growth-remediation model to a high of 18.9% for the no growth linear model and no growth rich get richer model. Finally, consistent with the hit rates, the kappa coefficients suggest that classification accuracy was higher for the linear and rich get richer growth models. The explanation for finding no false positive errors applies here as well.

Finally, false negative rates increase with growth amounts, as expected. As the distribution of Grade 3 reading proficiency moved to the right (relative to the distribution of Grade 2 proficiency), more and more examinees reach the Grade 3 proficient cut score, which remains fixed at 0.88 on the Grade 3 theta scale. This highlights the goal of this state assessment program and identifies a paradox: As regular instruction and intensive remediation become increasingly effective in improving the reading proficiency of third graders, the Grade 2 diagnostic test will increasingly overidentify students for remediation.

Classification accuracy results, accounting for errors in Grade 2 and 3 classifications.   Agreement between empirical classifications of examinees in Grade 2 and projected classifications of examinees in Grade 3, with measurement error accounted for in both classifications, is shown in Table 6. The results in this table can be compared to those in Table 5, in which measurement error was not accounted for in projected results. Table 6 contains percentages of examinees whose classification in Grades 2 and/or 3 was uncertain, as portrayed in Figure 1. The table also includes percentages of correct classifications (i.e., hits), incorrect classifications (i.e., false positive and negative errors), and the kappa coefficient, κ. Hits and classification errors were based on only those examinees not included in the five uncertain outcomes in Figure 1.

Table 6 contains several interesting results. First, Grade 3 classifications are uncertain for approximately one fourth to one third of the original 9,933 examinees whose Grade 3 data we simulated. These cases were counted in Table 5 as hits or classification errors. In Table 6 they illustrate the magnitude of uncertainty that is inherent in classifying examinees in longitudinal tracking of achievement growth: The measurement error for the Grade 2 and Grade 3 assessments is compounded, and the uncertainty that examinees are either above or below the Grade 2 cut score and, separately, above or below the Grade 3 cut score, compounds the uncertainty regarding which conjunctive categories they belong in across the two school years.

TABLE 6
Classification Accuracy of Grade 2 On Track Standard for 12 Hypothetical
Grade 3 Scenarios, Accounting for Measurement Error in the Grade 2 and
Grade 3 Assessments

			Classification Errors		
Growth Amount	*Uncertain*	*Hits*	*False Negative*	*False Positive*	κ
Linear growth model					
Negative	26.3	100.0	0.0	0.0	—
No	32.6	100.0	0.0	0.0	—
Low	36.2	99.1	0.0	0.9	.96
Moderate	33.2	90.3	0.0	9.7	.54
Remediation growth model					
Negative	28.8	100.0	0.0	0.0	—
No	35.7	100.0	0.0	0.0	—
Low	37.8	96.9	0.0	3.1	.81
Moderate	32.6	86.0	0.0	14.0	.28
Rich get richer growth model					
Negative	26.3	100.0	0.0	0.0	—
No	32.6	100.0	0.0	0.0	—
Low	36.2	99.1	0.0	0.9	.96
Moderate	33.2	90.3	0.0	9.7	.54

Note. κ = kappa coefficient; all other entries are percentages. Uncertain cases are removed from classification statistics. Sample sizes range between 2,483 and 3,277 in the Uncertain column (i.e., ¼ to ⅓ of the original simulated sample of 9,933); all other sample sizes do not include data for Uncertain classifications.

Second, since the data for uncertain classifications are removed from this analysis of classification accuracy and errors, hit rates in Table 6 are considerably higher than hit rates in Table 5. This is as expected, of course. Similarly, classification error rates in Table 6 are substantially reduced and kappa coefficients are substantially increased compared to Table 5. (Actually, the kappa for moderate growth in the remediation model is only slightly improved in Table 6.) As before, results for the linear and rich get richer growth models results are the same, and for the same reasons discussed previously.

The surprise in Table 6 is that all classification errors are false positive errors. In contrast, all classification errors in Table 5 were false negative errors. The explanation for this difference illustrates the clarity achieved by accounting for measurement error in estimating classification accuracy. The difference is also related to earlier discussions of the locations of the Grade 2 and 3 cut scores in their corresponding theta scales. It is most easily explained by examining the false positive errors in Table 6 more closely. We do so using Table 7.

Understanding the cause of the false positive errors in Table 6 using the breakdowns in Table 7 starts with the 1,922 students who were classified as clearly not

TABLE 7
Breakdown of False Positive Errors in Table 6, Showing Projected Grade 3
Classifications of Examinees for Observed Grade 2 Uncertain
and Clearly Not On Track Classifications

| | Grade 3 Projected | | | | | |
| | Uncertain | | Clearly Proficient | | Clearly Not Proficient | |
Grade 2 Clearly Not On Track[a]	%	N	%	N	%	N
Linear growth model and rich get richer model						
Low growth	58.1	1,117	3.0	58	38.9	747
Moderate growth	42.2	811	33.8	649	24.0	462
Remediation growth model						
Low growth	66.5	1,278	10.0	192	23.5	452
Moderate growth	39.5	759	49.0	941	11.6	222

Note. All rows sum to 1,922 cases and 100%.
[a]N = 1,922.

on track in Grade 2. Under the three growth models, few of these examinees are projected to reach clearly proficient in Grade 3 when projected growth is low; specifically, 3.0% for the linear and rich get richer growth models and 10.0% for the remediation model. When projected growth was moderate, the percentages of these examinees projected to reach clearly proficient increases substantially to 33.8 and 49.0%. These four percentages represent estimates, after measurement error is taken into account, of the numbers of students who can be expected to reach the proficient level in Grade 3, even though they were clearly not on track in Grade 2, if either low or moderate growth is achieved. It is clear that false positive classification error rates would be even higher than in Table 6, and false negative classification errors would be present, if uncertain cases had been included in the analyses.

SUMMARY AND DISCUSSION

In this article, we examined plausible scenarios for the classification accuracy of a Grade 2 diagnostic reading assessment that is linked to a Grade 3 reading achievement assessment using a vertical articulation process. We described the process of setting a Grade 3 proficient performance standard using the bookmark standard-setting method. Then we described the process of setting a Grade 2 on track performance standard using vertical articulation information as feedback to panelists. This feedback was intended to help panelists provide a Grade 2 performance standard that is vertically articulated with the Grade 3 performance standard. The vertical articulation process is a specific example of using social moderation to link performance standards across tests from adjacent grades. We used vertical articulation to link performance standards from these tests, rather than a statistical equating process to link scores from these tests because (a) differences in test content and item formats dictated against a test design that relied on overlapping items, and (b) reading skills—that is, the reading constructs—dictated against including overlapping items in each test.

It is important to remember the underlying assumption in vertical articulation of performance standards: Identifying Grade 2 students who are on track to reach proficient in Grade 3 assumes that students are on an achievement trajectory to reach that performance standard. Maintaining that achievement trajectory requires at a minimum that students will be taught and will learn the reading content standards that are assessed. We simulated Grade 3 data under three growth types (i.e., linear growth, remediation growth, and rich get richer growth) and four growth amounts (i.e., negative, zero, low, and moderate). We applied the Grade 3 reading assessment cut score in each of these 12 scenarios and examined the accuracy of the Grade 2 assessment in classifying examinees as on track to reach proficient on the Grade 3 assessment. We found that under these 12 hypothetical growth scenarios, the Grade 2 assessment was unlikely to misclassify examinees as false positives unless measurement error is taken into account. This is true, at least in situations like this one in which standard-setting panelists explicitly set a Grade 2 performance standard high enough to assure that all students who need remediation would be eligible for it in Grade 3, thus minimizing false positive classification errors. When we took measurement error into account, false positive classification errors did occur, even after we excluded all examinees whose classification was uncertain in either Grade 2 or Grade 3. Classification error rates would, of course, be higher than those reported in Table 6 if uncertain cases were included in the analyses.

Use of the uncertain category is helpful to understanding results in longitudinal tracking of examinee status in relation to performance standards. The NCLB Act (2001) reporting requirements are an example of such longitudinal tracking. If the effects of measurement error are not taken into account in classifying examinees— a typical practice in educational achievement test score reporting—the types and percentages of classification errors that can be detected are likely to be misleading. For example, Table 5 indicates that only false negative classification errors were present; in contrast, Table 6 indicates that only false positive classification errors occurred. A reporting system that includes uncertain classifications as well as classifications clearly above and below the performance standards is consistent with the actuality of measurement errors and would provide differentiated information to guide difficult decisions about allocating limited remediation resources in a targeted way. In fact, the state assessment program that provided the data for this study does report examinee results in these three categories in Kindergarten through Grade 2—grades not affected by the NCLB Act testing and reporting requirements.

Use of Grade 2 Test Results for Decision Making

The results of this study point to an important and complicated resource-use question: Which groups of students should receive the most intensive remediation, given that resources are limited? Using an uncertain category to identify examinees around the Grade 2 on track cut score can guide decisions. For example, examinees in the uncertain category, but just below the on track cut score perhaps would need less intensive and less resource-consuming remediation than examinees who are clearly not on track. More costly resources could be allocated for these latter students.[4] Further, examinees in the uncertain category but just above the on track cut score probably would benefit from less costly review of skills taught in Grade 2 to guard against erosion of those skills. (Of course, in practice, remediation decisions should be made using information from a range of sources, including teachers.)

In score reporting without the uncertain category, less information is available to guide decisions about allocating remediation resources. Examinees who just barely reach a performance standard often are viewed as marginal students who are just managing to meet standards. Although they may struggle academically, they typically may not get extra instructional attention because they are meeting standards, and other students are in greater need of attention. State departments of education and local schools and systems would have to explain to parents and teachers why some students who did not reach the on track level in Grade 2 will not receive the intensive remediation that others will receive. One solution could involve using additional reading proficiency information (e.g., teacher recommendations, additional individual reading assessment) to assign all students below the Grade 2 on track level to levels of different intensity of remediation services.

Potential consequences of not using an uncertain score reporting category are evident in the projected classification error rates in Table 5. For all three growth models, under the no growth scenario, the Grade 2 assessment overidentified 10% to 12% of second graders for intensive remediation in Grade 3; in the moderate growth scenario, overidentification is 21% to 24% (see Table 5). It is easy to envision the potential new costs and strains on school staff to provide intensive reading remediation for one tenth to one fifth of third graders beyond the numbers of students correctly identified for remediation without identifying the specifics of that remediation. In a school with 100 third graders in four classes of 25 students each,

---

[4]Or perhaps, the most costly and intensive resources would be allocated for students just below the on track cut score in an effort to help a school meet annual performance improvement goals.

each classroom teacher would have to manage standard instruction for students at grade level, provide remediation for students correctly classified below on track, and provide remediation for 2 to 5 additional students (i.e., 10–20 students shared evenly by four teachers) incorrectly classified below on track.

Implications for Vertical Moderation of Performance Standards

The vertical articulation process appears promising. It provides an alternative to creating overlapping test designs where such designs may be undesirable or insupportable. The Grade 2 on track reading standard appears to be linked reasonably well with the Grade 3 proficient reading standard, with the caveat that it may have overidentified students for remediation, as in Table 5, or underidentified them, as in Table 6.

These results may be plausibly generalizable to the performance standards for Kindergarten and Grade 1 reading assessments in this state assessment program. A single standard-setting panel articulated the reading standards for Kindergarten through Grade 2. Presumably, they applied the fairness concept (described previously) consistently to their judgments about on track standards for all three grades. Standard-setting panels in two other content areas discussed similar logic for articulating standards, as well. It may be reasonable to expect to see the overidentification of students for remediation that we found in these analyses (i.e., in Table 5) in other grades and content areas where use of the uncertain category is not allowed, at least for reporting results under the NCLB Act (2001) requirements.

REFERENCES

Berk, R. A. (1984). Selecting the index of reliability. In R. A. Berk (Ed.), *A guide to criterion-referenced test construction* (pp. 231–266). Baltimore, MD: The Johns Hopkins University Press.

Ercikan, K. (1997). Linking statewide tests to the National Assessment of Educational Progress: Accuracy of combining test results across states. *Applied Measurement in Education,* 10, 145–159.

Ferrara, S. (2003, June). Linking performance standards: Examples of judgmental approaches and possible applications to linking to NAEP. In A. Kolstad (Moderator), *Linking state assessment results to NAEP using statistical and judgmental methods.* Symposium conducted at the National Conference on Large Scale Assessment, San Antonio, TX.

Huynh, H., Meyer, P., & Barton, K. (2000). *Technical documentation for the South Carolina PACT-1999 tests.* (Available from the South Carolina State Department of Education, 1429 Senate St., Columbia, SC 29201.)

Johnson, E. G. (1998). *Linking the National Assessment of Educational Progress (NAEP) to the Third International Mathematics and Science Study (TIMSS): A technical report.* (Tech. Rep. No. 98–499). Washington, DC: U.S. Department of Education.

Johnson, E. G., Cohen, J., Chen, W-H., Jiang, T., & Zhang, Y. (2003). *2000 NAEP – 1999 TIMSS linking report.* (Available from the U.S. Department of Education, National Center for Education Statistics, 1990 K St., NW, Washington, DC 20006.)

Linn, R. L. (1993). Linking results of distinct assessments. *Applied Measurement in Education, 6*, 83–102.

Linn, R. L., & Kiplinger, V. L. (1995). Linking statewide tests to the National Assessment of Educational Progress: Stability of results. *Applied Measurement in Education, 8*, 135–155.

Lissitz, R., & Huynh, H. (2003). *Vertical equating for the Arkansas ACTAAP assessments: Issues and solutions in determination of adequate yearly progress and school accountability.* Unpublished manuscript.

McLaughlin, D., & Bandeira De Mello, V. (2003, June). Comparing state reading and math performance standards using NAEP. In A. Kolstad (Moderator), *Linking state assessment results to NAEP using statistical and judgmental methods.* Symposium conducted at the National Conference on Large Scale Assessment, San Antonio, TX.

Mislevy, R. J. (1992). *Linking educational assessments: Concepts, issues, methods, and prospects.* Princeton, NJ: Educational Testing Service.

Mitzel, H. C., Lewis, D. M., Patz, R. J., & Green, D. R. (2001). The bookmark procedure: Psychological perspectives. In G. J. Cizek (Ed.), *Setting performance standards: Concepts, methods, and perspectives.* (pp. 249–281). Mahwah, NJ: Lawrence Erlbaum Associates, Inc.

National Research Council. (1998). *Uncommon measures: Equivalence and linkage among educational tests.* Washington, DC: National Academy Press.

No Child Left Behind Act of 2001, Pub. L. Number 107–110, 20 U.S.C.6301 (2002).

Slinde, J. A., & Linn, R. L. (1977). Vertically equated tests: Fact or phantom? *Journal of Educational Measurement, 14*, 23–32.

APPLIED MEASUREMENT IN EDUCATION, *18*(1), 61–81

Criteria for Standard Setting from the Sponsor's Perspective

William D. Schafer

Department of Measurement, Statistics, and Evaluation
University of Maryland

Two concerns related to setting performance standards on educational assessments are discussed. First, criteria for a standard-setting process from the point of view of a standard-setting sponsor, called here "institutional criteria," are developed using a state department of education as an example. Four institutional criteria are proposed: (a) consistency with policy goals, (b) legal defensibility, (c) generation of assets for support, and (d) efficiency. Some steps sponsors may take toward meeting these criteria are introduced by reviewing, and in some cases elaborating on, Hambleton's (2001) 20 questions from the perspective of the 4 criteria. Second, the concept of vertical moderation of performance standards is reviewed, and considerations that can lead to different choices for moderation of standards are explored. Realistic state data are used to illustrate some of these choices. How moderated standards may be consistent with the 4 institutional criteria is discussed.

PERSPECTIVES ON STANDARD SETTING

Standard setting (or more precisely, setting cut scores that operationalize standards) was criticized as too arbitrary (Glass, 1978) and has even been called "the Achilles' heel of the high-stakes testing business" (Glass, 2003, p. 102). In contrast, Mehrens and Cizek (2001), in their concluding chapter in a book devoted to standard setting, stated that "the technology of setting performance standards is ... well developed" (p. 484) and Cizek (personal communication, July 6, 2004) believes that "nearly all psychometricians now agree that standard setting is not an arbitrary endeavor but a fairly well-developed technology for applying human

---

Requests for reprints should be sent to William D. Schafer, Department of Measurement, Statistics, and Evaluation, University of Maryland, College of Education, College Park, MD 20742–1115. E-mail: wschafer@umd.edu

judgment in reasonable, reproducible, and defensible ways." Its prevalence, if nothing else, suggests that no acceptable alternative has been found to satisfy the need for judgments of whether achievement in a specified domain is sufficient for some adjective such as *basic*, *proficient*, or *advanced*.

The popularity of standard-setting procedures and subsequent decision making implies that it is useful to consider criteria for the success of a standard-setting event. There are at least four perspectives from which criteria might be approached. I list them here in order of increasing usefulness to the sponsoring agency.

Definitional Perspective

To be called performance standards, there must be operationally defined, mutually exclusive, exhaustive ordered categories and a decision process based on one or more assessments to place students in those categories. This is not very helpful in determining whether the quality of the decision rule is adequate.

Psychometric Perspective

Standards result in categorizations of students, and inferences are drawn from those categories about students and about the programs that, at least in part, are responsible for those categorizations. As such, they form a scale that can be evaluated using the well-known criteria of reliability, validity, and utility. Kane (2001) took this perspective in his discussion of approaches to validating inferences made from categorizations using cut scores based on standards. The definitional approach seems subsumed by the psychometric.

Legal Perspective

Performance standards are a part of a decision-making process. Assuming the decisions have importance (i.e., stakes, which imply the possibility of harm), the process may be held to criteria that courts have determined are crucial for legal acceptability. Considerations such as equal protection (fairness) and due process (including adequate notice) have been applied through judicial proceedings to high-stakes decisions about students (Phillips, 2001) and may in the future be applied to decisions about schools (Parkes & Stevens, 2003). Along with the criterion of having a legitimate purpose, the legal perspective has been proposed by Cizek (1993) and further explored by Camilli, Cizek, & Lugg (2001). I place these criteria here on the continuum as more useful to the sponsoring organization because they subsume the psychometric criteria.

The Institutional Perspective

The four general criteria proposed in this section seem most salient from the point of view of the organization sponsoring (and likely having the eventual responsibility to implement) the performance standards (and cut scores, which are part of the standards' operationalization). They also seem to subsume the other three perspectives. I describe briefly the four institutional criteria follwing. I then explore their implications.

Consistency with policy goals.   Standards are developed for a purpose, although there may be a variety of goals that different stakeholders expect them to serve. As Kane (2001) pointed out, standards are justified in part by their relationship with legitimate goals. This suggests that the sponsoring organization, or legitimate authority (Haertel, 2002) has intended outcomes (perhaps unstated) that can be used as criteria for making judgments about the eventual success of the standard-setting process. It is against this criterion that the concept of moderation of standards (Lissitz & Huynh, 2003; discussed later) seems to fit best because moderation may or may not be implied by the policy goals of the sponsoring organization.

Legal defensibility.   To the extent that important, high-stakes decisions are made, there is the likelihood that actions will be taken that subject the standard-setting process to an evaluation based on legal principles. Some of these have been mentioned previously. It is natural that the sponsoring organization should desire as much assurance as possible that its use of the resulting standards will be upheld if challenged in court.

Generation of assets.   The sponsoring organization has a need for means in order to achieve public or political support for the use of the cut scores that operationalize its standards. Assets for acceptance by stakeholder groups may be of several types, including persons involved in the process and outside experts (e.g., psychometric and content-area professionals), materials such as technical manuals, and research into such aspects as consistency with other indicators and consequences for students and for programs. The latter might generate data to evaluate consistency with policy goals where they may exist (I use illustrative state data as an example).

Efficient use of resources.   The sponsoring organization will want to spend its resources wisely. There may even be a need to account publicly for how prudent it has been.

IMPLICATIONS OF THE INSTITUTIONAL CRITERIA

Are the institutional criteria suggested previously consistent with or do they differ from current thinking about "best practice" in standard setting? What do the institutional criteria imply for the conduct of standard-setting studies? Hambleton (2001) posed 20 questions that appear to cover a broad range of activities that various authors have determined to be useful in standard setting. I use them here, restated as topics and suggestions, as a comprehensive and up-to-date list of recommendations to which the institutional criteria might be applied. As seems appropriate, I then elaborate each as suggested by the institutional criteria to see if the criteria are helpful. I raise two additional issues from the standpoint of the four institutional criteria.

I review Hambleton's (2001) 20 evaluation criteria from the perspective of the sponsoring organization in the following sections of this article. The model used is that of a state department of education interested in setting standards for school and student accountability. Clearly other organizations, such as professional certification boards and national and international testing associations, are also sponsoring organizations for which the institutional criteria may well be useful. Testing the application of the institutional criteria to these other agencies is beyond the scope of this article but would be a helpful expansion.

CRITERIA FOR STANDARD SETTING

The institutional perspective suggests that two topics that appear outside of Hambleton's (2001) compendium be introduced before those proposed by Hambleton. These are (a) goals clarification and (b) constituent identification. I add them here because they are best implemented in the beginning phases of a standard-setting project.

Goals Clarification

So that the resulting standards are consistent with the sponsoring agency's policy goals, it is necessary that those goals be explicitly stated. Although this activity may be accomplished during or even after the panels have completed their work, it seems more helpful if goals clarification were to be done beforehand. Only then can the goals be used to make judgments about the adequacy of the standard-setting process.

Constituent Identification

It is important to note that Hambleton (2001) did not specify an audience for his questions (i.e., those who he intended should be convinced that the answers to the questions are satisfactory). Generating assets for achieving public support is easier if the public constituencies who need to be convinced are already defined. Knowing what each will want to know and what evidence each will find convincing should be suggestive of the sorts of assets that need to be generated to lead to their support.

Composition of the Panel

Hambleton (2001) was concerned about whether the groups who ought to be represented were represented by qualified individuals. Because it goes directly to validity, this is primarily a legal defensibility issue. Haertel (2002) suggested that an array of stakeholder groups should have impact on both the content and achievement standards that are implemented through the use of cut scores. However, it may also be considered a development of assets issue because the composition of the panel may be judged in terms of the groups who would best make the case to the public that the standards should be supported. Besides educators, the producers of graduates, those who further educate or employ graduates would be natural groups to consider. This suggests including employers and university educators in setting standards for high school students (perhaps with an emphasis on those who employ and train those candidates who are minimally successful) and including teachers from higher grades when setting standards for elementary and middle school students. Those who provide resources to the sponsor (e.g., political leaders, who also help shape public opinion) are another group whose support would be useful, along with persons who have credibility in making recommendations about special populations, such as advocates for persons with disabilities, the limited-English proficient, and demographic minorities, especially those who may be adversely affected by the assessment program. Whether including these groups is feasible within the resources of the sponsor and whether including them on panels is the best way to generate their helpful support are open questions, but including them on panels can be a viable way to accomplish the purpose.

Size of the Panel

Hambleton (2001) noted that the panel should be large enough to represent all appropriate stakeholder groups (while assuring that the subject-matter knowledge of all persons is sufficient to enable them to make the needed ratings). Including persons from each of the groups identified previously is likely to stretch the capacity of many sponsors, and compromises may be necessary. When that happens, a process to make these compromises that will demonstrate that all relevant constituencies were allowed an effective voice in reaching a consensus on participation decisions could be helpful to the sponsor in promoting the eventual outcome.

Size is also a statistical issue. A cut score that results from the standard-setting procedure could be thought to estimate the cut score that would in theory result from repeated replications of the procedure with randomly equivalent samples. The standard error of that process is estimable (see the next section) and decreases as sample size increases.

Estimation of Standard Error Across Panels

Two types of standard errors are commonly reported in standard-setting studies: standard errors of panels and standard errors of measurement. The latter are available from psychometric analyses that are independent of the standard-setting study. Standard errors of panels, which are the focus of Hambleton's (2001) question, are commonly estimated through subdividing the panel into two or more subpanels. In practice, the two standard errors are often combined and used in deliberations subsequent to a given study to provide a range of values (e.g., the recommendation plus or minus two of the combined standard errors) that may be used in making adjustments.

Funding Adequacy

As Hambleton (2001) pointed out, standard setting can consume significant resources. The greater the importance of the decisions made using the standards, the more justifiable are the expenses needed for the process. Hambleton's concern about sufficiency of funding is appropriate. However, virtually any sponsor has obligations to others to spend resources wisely. Developing a justification that balances costs against value of the product for the level of funding committed to the standard-setting procedure and ancillary activities could provide useful documentation that the efficiency criterion was met.

Field Testing

Hambleton (2001) noted that although uncommon, field testing the study can and likely will yield revisions to the process, and thus it is formative. The tryout can be evaluated against the four institutional criteria (or the topics mentioned here). Including at least five perspectives in the evaluation of the tryout would be helpful: (a) policy groups (for match with their goals), (b) legal staff (for legal defensibility), (c) methodologists (as respected professionals whose opinions are useful for asset generation), (d) representatives of the public and other stakeholders mentioned previously so that other members of the public will believe that all important perspectives were represented (useful for asset generation), and (e) the tryout participants themselves so that those most closely involved in the judgment process have positive opinions (also useful for asset generation).

Appropriateness of the Method

Not only should the method be described in enough detail that it can be replicated (suggested by Hambleton, 2001), but considerations that led to the choice of method in the first place can also become a material asset in communicating the results to stakeholders.

Preparation of the Participants

Hambleton (2001) described two aspects of preparation: (a) an explanation of the purposes and uses of the assessments and (b) exposure to the assessments and how they are scored. Participants who are well prepared should be more likely to support the standard-setting results, whereas participants who were not aware of the nature and consequences of the assessment program might very well disavow the eventual standards when they realize they were making judgments for a context they did not fully understand.

This situation seems akin to the informed consent process in doing research with human participants; the participants must be aware of all factors that might affect their recommendations. When are the assessments administered? What are the stakes for the student? What are the stakes for the school and/or district? Who makes decisions about consequences, how are they made, and when are they reported? When do these consequences begin? What materials exist or are being developed to help teachers reach their and their students' instructional goals? Are there remediation opportunities? What is new and what is unchanged from that which currently exists? Knowing answers to questions such as these should increase the likelihood that the participants will make better recommendations (i.e., recommendations that are consistent with policy needs) and will support the standards that are eventually set, thus becoming more valuable as assets for generating public acceptance. To this end, it would be helpful to have the script (or talking points) used to brief the participants incorporated into any field testing.

Understanding features of the test development process would also be helpful to the participants in their deliberations as well as useful in helping them to act as assets after the procedure is completed. Among these are the process used to develop the content standards, how the test items are developed and field tested (including reviews, both substantive and statistical, of items for quality, sensitivity, and bias), and how the tests are constructed, administered, scored, scaled, and reported.

Collection of Panel Qualifications and Demographics

Hambleton (2001) noted that information about the participants' qualifications and relevant demographics, as well as their motivation for participation, is needed for documentation. Other relevant information that can enhance public support is how the participants were chosen and solicited.

Exposure of the Participants to the Assessment

Hambleton recommended that the participants actually complete the assessment under conditions that simulate the actual testing and most standard-setting procedures now include this feature, although it can be a challenge for some assessment administration methods (e.g., computer adaptive testing) or test lengths (e.g., tests that are given over long periods of time or in more than one session). Yet participants need an understanding of the actual testing context and tasks that students face.

Training of Participants on the Standard-Setting Method

The adequacy with which participants are trained to perform their tasks is crucial. Hambleton (2001) also noted that participants themselves and an independent evaluator are two sources of data that can be used in current as well as in future standard-setting studies to evaluate the quality of that training. Checking participants' understanding throughout the process and having personnel available to correct misperceptions can lead to improved judgments and can leave participants with a more positive impression, enhancing their value as advocates for the standards.

Development of Performance Category Descriptions

Hambleton (2001) noted that the use of agreed-upon performance category descriptions by participants in the standard-setting process is a recently introduced and positive feature. Although it is reasonable that a consensus about performance category descriptions reduces interjudge variability, several options exist. There are at least four important (interrelated) dimensions in developing performance category descriptions: target, specificity, source, and timing.

Target. Performance category descriptions are intended to specify what students in each of the categories are expected to know and be able to do. However, each category is actually a range of degrees of achievement. As Lewis and Green (1997) pointed out, some standard-setting procedures target the average student(s) within the range and others, sometimes called borderline descriptions, target the lowest-performing student(s). Other locations are possible, though less likely. Lewis and Green recommended that performance-level descriptions target the minimum levels of performance in each category, in part so that the description represents knowledge and abilities common to all students in that range.

Specificity.   Category descriptions may be content-specific or general. General descriptions (e.g., "ready to study the material at the next level") do not describe what examinees know and can do and therefore require elaboration. They are often used as preliminary category (or achievement-level) descriptions at the beginning of a standard-setting study. Content-specific descriptions, such as those that are almost universally developed by the end of the study, specify the understandings and skills that examinees in each category should possess. Although sometimes developed by the participants, these have on occasion been developed by an outside group, making the participants responsible only for judgments about which of the category descriptions is represented by a given student performance.

Source.   If content-specific performance category descriptions are developed prior to (or perhaps during) the study, then there may be some group other than the standard-recommending panel that is involved. In that event, issues related to the size and composition of the description-recommending panel parallel those of the standard-recommending panel. The stability of their judgments is also a (researchable) question that naturally arises. On the other hand, if content-specific category descriptions are developed during the study, then the standard-setting panel becomes (or is likely to be) the description-recommending panel.

Timing.   Preliminary category descriptions may be developed prior to or during the standard-setting recommending study. If the latter, they may be developed at the end or while the study is in progress. Developing them during the study can be attractive. Indeed, continually refining the category descriptions (or borderline descriptions) may be an effective way for facilitators to focus the discussions that arise in panels at each of the rounds (Loomis & Bourque, 2001).

Utility of Feedback to Participants Between Rounds of Judgments

For iterative standard-setting processes—which most are—this topic refers to how feedback was presented to the participants and how well they were able to make use of it. Hambleton (2001) suggested that this topic could be evaluated in two ways: postquestionnaires and low recommended cut-score standard errors. This topic seems more associated with the generation of assets and legal defensibility criteria.

Efficiency

There are two aspects to efficiency. First, as Hambleton (2001) noted, the study should proceed smoothly. The materials should be clear, participant time should be used effectively, and transitions should flow easily. These are aspects that are most closely associated with the generation of assets criterion and for which a field test can be especially helpful.

Another aspect to efficiency is effective use of the sponsor's resources. For example, not all questions and assumptions need be addressed in each standard-setting implementation. Insights developed from research in similar contexts are becoming more and more available as the field matures and these can be used to justify commonly accepted methods. For example, it is sometimes recommended that multiple approaches be used in standard setting to show that the results generalize across methods. However, including multiple approaches in each study can be and likely is beyond the resources of most sponsors (which is another way of saying that the funds could be used more effectively in other ways). Instead, literature that evaluates consistency between procedures could be noted in a technical manual. The efficiency criterion suggests broadening this topic to include cost effectiveness.

Grounding With Performance Data

Hambleton (2001) recommended that participants have data on how well examinees performed at the item (e.g., p values) and test (e.g., deciles) levels. Hambleton suggested that the goal should be to provide helpful but not directive information that makes judges aware of typical levels of responding by examinee groups. This topic is closely related to the next.

Use of Impact Data

Participants are usually given data that show the consequences of their interim recommended cut points on examinees and/or examinee groups. Hambleton (2001) recommended that the participants be instructed on how to use the data so that they could decide whether they need to revise their recommendations on the basis of reasonableness.

There may be a tension within panels, particularly if the participants have been chosen broadly. Some members may tend to try to ground their recommendations with consequences and others with content-related understandings and skills. Facilitators are commonly asked to remind participants that they are being asked to base their recommendations on comparisons of the content standards with examinee descriptions. However, impact information, once given, is difficult to ignore, and informed negotiations between participants with different orientations could actually be a healthy process toward reaching publicly supportable performance standards and assets to help generate that support.

How Final Standards Were Achieved

One or more groups normally review final standards following the participants' recommendations. Hambleton (2001) noted that whatever steps and processes are used, they should be clear to the participants and explainable to important boards and agencies. Awareness on the part of the judges of the possibility that their recommendations will be amended seems important to maintaining their good will following the study and therefore their value as assets.

Participant Evaluation

Hambleton (2001) pointed out that positive participant evaluations about their training, the method, and the category descriptions can be used in defending the performance standards, a direct instance of the development of assets criterion. Ensuring that they have ample opportunities to raise concerns about any of these aspects during the study can make positive evaluations more likely. As long as the participants do not learn anything new following the study that might have affected their recommendations, they are likely to continue to support the resulting standards and thus continue to be useful in gaining public acceptance.

Validity Evidence for the Performance Standards

Kane (2001) defined two characteristics on which the use of cut scores is based. He called them the policy assumption (that the standards are appropriate for the decision, which can be associated with the consistency with policy goals criterion) and the descriptive assumption (that each cut score can be used to separate examinees into those who do and those who do not meet the performance standard, which is associated with the legal defensibility and generation of assets criteria). Hambleton (2001) suggested that validity evidence in support of these assumptions should be developed along Kane's three evidentiary sources: procedural (quality of the design and implementation of the standard-setting procedure), internal (reliability of classifications), and external (evaluating classification decisions based on other relevant evidence about student performance). As Kane noted, consequential evidence (e.g., competencies or lack thereof on the part of successful candidates, presence or absence of unfair adverse impact) is needed as well. Although these recommendations are consistent with the psychometric perspective, they are no less important from the institutional perspective. This topic is clearly broad and seems to apply to all the institutional criteria except efficiency.

Documentation of the Process

As Hambleton (2001) noted, all the topics thus far can be evaluated individually, and a technical report should be prepared to document success. The report, itself can become a material asset for the sponsor. This task could be the responsibility of the sponsor (especially because several decisions that need to be documented are commonly determined even before a request for proposals [RFP] is issued, such as the general standard-setting approach), or the sponsor may make the report the sole responsibility of a contractor, with or without specifications about what is to be included. If the sponsor retains responsibility, a straightforward way to accomplish that could be to assign the development of the technical report to in-house personnel from the beginning, with sections to be completed by the contractor(s) as noted in the RFP. It would be helpful for the assessment community to develop recommendations about what material to include and how to format it. Possible starting points for formatting would be to use the evaluation criteria or the topics explored in this article as sections for the document.

Effective Communication of Standards

The performance of examinees who fall in each of the performance categories is usually communicated using content-specific category descriptions. Hambleton (2001) suggested that although these category descriptions may be sufficient, exemplar items, either of the categories or at the borderlines, could enhance communication of what examinees in each category know and can do. Material and people used to communicate the standards become assets for public acceptance, and data showing their reasonableness and consistency with other information are research assets.

Most assessments are actually composites of highly but not perfectly correlated content strands and the use of a cut score defined on a single scale therefore represents a compensatory decision rule. Yet performance categories are typically presented as if the rule were conjunctive (i.e., students in this category can do all of these things). It would be helpful for educators, candidates, and the public (as well as the participants) to understand the compensatory nature of the use of a single cut score between categories.

MODERATION OF STANDARDS

The institutional criteria seem reasonable when compared with Hambleton's (2001) questions from a theoretical perspective, but do they help in evaluating a standard-setting orientation? I use them to review the method known as vertical moderation of standards.

Lissitz and Huynh (2003) proposed vertically moderated standards (VMS) for statewide tests. After reviewing the current status of vertical scaling from the perspectives of validity and practicality, Lissitz and Huynh concluded that vertical scales are too problematic to recommend for many current situations in which they have been considered. Using the development of cut scores in South Carolina as an example, their process for VMS as an alternative to vertical scaling seems to have these elements:

1. Determine a policy definition for proficiency (or whatever category the cut score is intended to operationalize as the minimum). This is done separately for different content areas. The policy definition should include forward-looking elements such as that the student should be able to maintain the same level of proficiency in the next year.
2. The material presented to the participants should include the curriculum in at least 2 years (the target grade and the subsequent or previous grade), the actual test items and blueprints, and scatter plots displaying the relationships between the 2 years that will help maintain (or at least understand) normative (in)consistency between the standards.
3. In the event that not all grades are available for standard setting (e.g., because development of assessments in some grades lags development in others), Lissitz and Huynh (2003) allow setting cut scores by interpolation or extrapolation of proficiency-level achievement rates (impacts) to intermediate assessments.
4. Within margin-of-error bands resulting from confidence intervals generated using standard errors of the participant-recommended cut scores, adjustments may be made based on policy considerations when the consequences justify them.
5. Annual studies should be conducted to validate the standards.

A Hypothetical Example of VMS

The promise of VMS is to be able to make inferences about growth in student achievement without vertical scaling in place. How does this concept fare when judged according to the criteria for standard setting developed from the institutional perspective? That question is discussed using examples of realistic outcomes of standard-setting procedures in four simulated but realistic states: East Pacific, North Mexico, South Canada, and West Atlantic.

Figures 1 through 8 show the hypothetical percentages of students above the minimum (i.e., proficient) cut for making No Child Left Behind (NCLB) Act (2001) decisions in reading and math for the four states. Also shown are hypothetical percentages of students above the cuts for the most recent National Assessment of Educational Progress (NAEP) results for the basic and proficient levels (upper and lower dotted lines, respectively). Finally, hypothetical ranges of two standard errors (measurement and standard-setting combined) above and below the panels' recommended cuts are included (the dashed lines below and above the solid line, respectively). Typical of actual states, data for all grade levels were assumed to be unavailable, so for all these series, linear interpolation and extrapolation were used

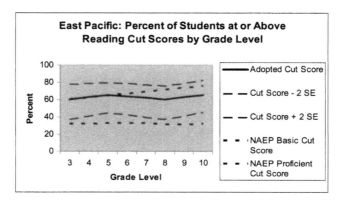

FIGURE 1   Reading results for East Pacific.

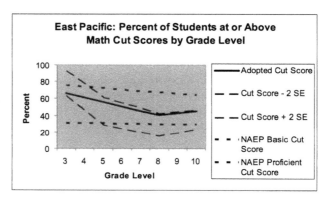

FIGURE 2   Math results for East Pacific.

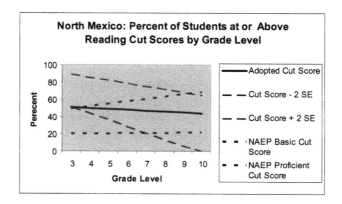

FIGURE 3   Reading results for North Mexico

74

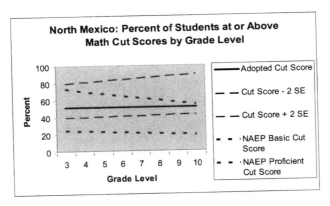

FIGURE 4   Math results for North Mexico.

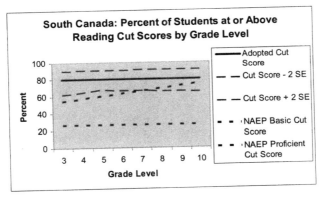

FIGURE 5   Reading results for South Canada.

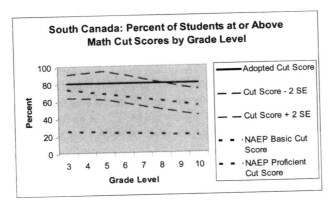

FIGURE 6   Math results for South Canada.

75

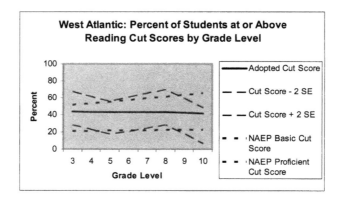

FIGURE 7   Reading results for West Atlantic.

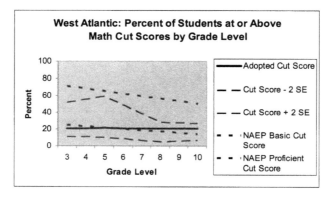

FIGURE 8   Math results for West Atlantic.

to generate results for all grade levels, 3 through 10. It should be noted that a policy using interpolation and extrapolation would be unfair to Lissitz and Huynh (2003) because the process they recommend involves thoughtful judgments about annual relations and these quantitative methods are to be substituted only when necessary (see point 3 previously). The figures are used here for illustration only, and ficti-tious names are used. Nevertheless, they are intended to be realistic and to portray fairly the challenges typical of states across the country (it would be straightfor-ward to construct such a figure for a real state, given the appropriate data). In these diverse contexts, I turn to a discussion of each of the four institutional criteria.

   Consistency with policy goals.   The need to include forward-looking ele-ments in the characterizations of proficiency levels is not necessarily a part of a state's expressed policy goals. Nevertheless, it is almost surely consistent with the state's general intent. The assumption that standards should be moderated through interpolation and extrapolation seems a bit more problematic because there may be other considerations than smoothness of pass rates. There was remarkable consistency across grade levels in three of the states (North Mexico, South Canada, and West Atlantic), but the rates were less smooth in East Pacific. Perhaps the apparent lack of moderation in East Pacific represents some beliefs of the state, such as about the difficulties of the content standards across the grades, the comparative rigor of the performance standards, the progression of learning over time, or the relative success of current instruction at different grade levels.

Whether cuts for content areas should be set together may also be an issue for a state to consider from a policy perspective. In the figures, the percentages above cut were about the same for reading and math for two states (North Mexico and South Canada), but reading cuts seem more lenient than math cuts in two others (East Pacific and West Atlantic). Moderation across content areas may be just as important as moderation across grade levels.

A reasonable conclusion is that moderation may be a policy goal, but it competes with others. Although lack of moderation, either across grades or across contents, can lead to unbalanced consequences and asymmetric remedies, those outcomes may be consistent with policy goals. Moderation does not appear to be an end in itself.

Legal defensibility. Of course, the proposed moderation process has not been tested against the legal criteria of legitimacy, due process, and fairness. Can one anticipate some issues that may arise in comparison with another approach, such as setting standards using one of the currently accepted procedures? Legitimacy seems not to be a problem because the authority and purpose of the agency is the same whether or not vertical moderation is used. Similarly, fairness should not be impacted differently. However, due process may be of concern. Standards could be set based almost exclusively on normative data. Inferences about the knowledge and skills of examinees would not then have the support of professional and other stakeholder evaluations of the curriculum, its alignment with the assessments, and the achievement-level descriptions of the performance categories, including remediation recommendations. If moderation is used to set cut scores, it is likely that this area is in significant need of being addressed, such as in the program of research that Lissitz and Huynh (2003) recommend as a step in implementing their suggestions.

Generation of assets. Earlier, assets were broadly classified into three types: persons, materials, and research studies. If a state were to develop some of its cut scores using vertical moderation, at least some of these assets would not exist. In this analysis, I describe some of the assets that each of the four states might have had available at each of the grade level and content combinations to use for public acceptance.

One assumes the contractors in each state documented in technical reports at the end of the study the characteristics and beliefs of the persons who were involved. Whether those beliefs were maintained after the study is an open question. Additionally, one assumes each state incorporated an outside technical advisory group that reviewed the procedures and provided evaluative commentary. These reports provide material assets for the state.

Technical reports often provide details about the development and variability of the recommended standards. These data can be compared with the adopted standards to gauge whether the cut scores actually used are consistent with the recommendations of the judges. As seen in the figures, each state in both contents set cut scores that were within two combined standard errors of the committee recommendations, with one exception (South Canada in math at the two higher grades, which are extrapolated values in the simulation). Documentation of consistency between the participants' recommendations and the adopted standards is a valuable material asset.

In addition to the technical report of the standard-setting study, technical manuals for the tests, and the decision rules used at the state level are needed. For example, a state's rules for determining adequate yearly progress are part of its policy implementation and are thus needed for an evaluation of the state's accountability program, whether by an internal process or by interested members of the public. Although they are independent of the standard-setting procedure implementation, documenting these points can provide additional material assets that would be helpful for a state.

The figures also include an example of a research outcome. In each case, simulated results of state NAEP for the basic and proficient performance levels (and above) were plotted (with interpolation and extrapolation, used here only for purposes of illustration). This allows a comparison between the state's achievement levels and those of a credible external assessment. Although these comparisons may suffer from different degrees of alignment between the state NAEP frameworks and a state's content standards, they do provide evidence that the public might use in order to evaluate the rigor of a state's performance standards.

These comparisons reveal some sharp differences among the hypothetical states shown in Figures 1 through 8. In South Canada, the adopted cuts for both contents appear more lenient than NAEP basic. In North Mexico and East Pacific, they appear between NAEP basic and NAEP proficient. The cuts for reading in West Atlantic are also between NAEP basic and proficient, but for math they are approximately as severe as NAEP proficient. Although the implications of these different degrees of rigor for educational impacts remain to be seen, members of the public would likely place their own values on such comparisons, and thus, there are implications of these comparisons for public acceptance of the cut scores that operationalize the performance standards. These comparisons would be possible whether or not the cut points were determined using moderation.

Efficient use of resources.   While gathering data to support the cost-effectiveness of a standard-setting study would be helpful to the sponsoring organization and is possible (e.g., by comparison with other organizations that have conducted similar studies), the efficiency introduced via the competitive bidding process required in most states when contracting with an external vendor for testing services may be sufficient for most audiences. It is an open question whether the cost saving provided by developing VMS rather than conducting studies at all grade levels is sufficient to compensate for the loss of person and material assets that result from the studies.

CONCLUSIONS

Guided by earlier work on goals for implementation of such activities, I proposed four criteria for standard setting from the perspective of the institution that will use the standards. The four criteria are (a) consistency with policy goals, (b) legal defensibility, (c) generation of assets (including people, materials, and research evidence), and (d) efficient use of resources. I reviewed the comprehensiveness and utility of these four goals using Hambleton's (2001) extensive list of questions that should be addressed in any standard-setting implementation. It was found that Hambleton's suggestions could be supported in terms of the goals. Further, the goals led to an expanded list of recommendations for standard-setting studies in several areas and to two new issues that were not raised by Hambleton.

Although I developed and discussed them from the perspective of a state department of education, whether the four criteria may apply equivalently in other contexts is an open question. It is possible that one or more might not apply well or that they might apply but in different ways. For example, elements needed for legal defensibility might be different for a private as opposed to a public sponsor.

There appear to be implications of all four of the institutional criteria for the advisability of using vertical moderation to establish cut scores for performance categories. Vertical moderation is certainly more efficient, but whether that is sufficient to offset the loss of assets is debatable. The consistency between VMSs and policy goals is an open question that should be addressed explicitly in each application because the goals themselves are likely to be idiosyncratic. Whether the justification of VMS is sufficient to withstand legal challenge is another unanswered question. Finally, I suggested horizontal moderation (across content areas at the same grade) as a reasonable concept for policymakers to consider in relation to their policy goals.

ACKNOWLEDGMENT

This project was partially funded by the Maryland State Department of Education (MSDE) under a contract to the Maryland Assessment Research Center for Education Success (MARCES). The opinions expressed do not necessarily reflect those of MSDE or of MARCES.

REFERENCES

Camilli, G., Cizek, G. J., & Lugg, C. A. (2001). Psychometric theory and the validation of performance standards: History and future perspectives. In G. J. Cizek (Ed.), *Setting performance standards: Concepts, methods, and perspectives* (pp. 445–475). Mahwah, NJ: Lawrence Erlbaum Associates, Inc.

Cizek, G. J. (1993). Reconsidering standards and criteria. *Journal of Educational Measurement, 30,* 93–106.

Glass, G. V. (1978). Standards and criteria. *Journal of Educational Measurement, 15,* 237–261.

Glass, G. V. (2003). Cut-scores: Where do they come from? In Boston, C., L. M. Rudner, L. J. Walker, & L. Crouch (Eds.), *What reporters need to know about test scores* (pp. 93–109). Washington, DC: Education Writers Asociation.

Haertel, E. H. (2002). Standard setting as a participatory process: Implications for validation of standards-based accountability programs. *Educational Measurement: Issues and Practice, 21*(1), 16–22.

Hambleton, R. K. (2001). Setting performance standards on educational assessments and criteria for evaluating the process. In G. J. Cizek (Ed.), *Setting performance standards: Concepts, methods, and perspectives* (pp. 89–116). Mahwah, NJ: Lawrence Erlbaum Associates, Inc.

Kane, M. T. (2001). So much remains the same: Conception and status of validation in setting standards. In G. J. Cizek (Ed.), *Setting performance standards: Concepts, methods, and perspectives* (pp. 53–88). Mahwah, NJ: Lawrence Erlbaum Associates, Inc.

Lewis, D. M. & Green, D. R. (1997, June). *The validity of performance level descriptors.* Paper presented at the 1997 Council of Chief State School Officers National Conference on Large Scale Assessment, Colorado Springs, CO.

Lissitz, R. W. & Huynh, H. (2003). Vertical equating for state assessments: Issues and solutions in determination of adequate yearly progress and school accountability. *Practical Assessment, Research & Evaluation, 8*(10). Retrieved February 5, 2004 from http://PAREonline.net/getvn.asp?v=8&n=10

Loomis, S. C. & Bourque, M. L. (2001). From tradition to innovation: Standard setting on the National Assessment of Educational Progress. In G. J. Cizek (Ed.), *Setting performance standards: Concepts, methods, and perspectives* (pp. 175–217). Mahwah, NJ: Lawrence Erlbaum Associates, Inc.

Mehrens, W. A., & Cizek, G. J. (2001). Standard setting and the public good: Benefits accrued and anticipated. In G. J. Cizek (Ed.). *Setting performance standards: Concepts, methods, and perspectives* (pp. 477–485). Mahwah, NJ: Lawrence Erlbaum Associates, Inc.

No Child Left Behind Act of 2001, Pub. L. No. 107–110 (2002). Retrieved on August 2, 2004 from http://www.ed.gov/policy/elsec/leg/esea02/107–110.pdf

Parkes, J. & Stevens, J. (2003). Legal issues in school accountability systems. *Applied Measurement in Education, 16*, 141–158.

Phillips, S. E. (2001). Legal issues in standard setting for k-12 programs. In G. J. Cizek (Ed.), *Setting performance standards: Concepts, methods, and perspectives* (pp. 411–426). Mahwah, NJ: Lawrence Erlbaum Associates, Inc.

APPLIED MEASUREMENT IN EDUCATION, *18*(1), 83–98

A Case Study of Vertically Moderated Standard Settting for a State Science Assessment Program

Chad W. Buckendahl
Buros Center for Testing
University of Nebraska-Lincoln

Huynh Huynh
College of Education
University of South Carolina

Theresa Siskind
South Carolina Department of Education
Columbia, South Carolina

Joseph Saunders
South Carolina Department of Education
Columbia, South Carolina

Under the adequate yearly progress requirements of the No Child Left Behind (NCLB) Act (2001), states are currently faced with the challenge of demonstrating continuous improvement in student performance in reading and mathematics. Beginning in 2007 to 2008, science will be required as a component of the NCLB Act. This article describes South Carolina's elementary science assessments and its approach to setting achievement levels on those tests. A description of how the state developed a system of vertically moderated standards across the range of grades covered by the tests is provided. Included in the process are standard-setting activities, Technical Advisory Committee deliberations, State Department of Education final decisions, and data provided to the state's Board of Education for information purposes. Recommendations for practice are also provided.

Requests for reprints should be sent to: Chad W. Buckendahl, Buros Center for Testing, 21 TEAC, University of Nebraska, Lincoln, NE 68588-0353. E-mail: cbuck1@unl.edu

Under the adequate yearly progress requirements of the No Child Left Behind (NCLB) Act (2001) legislation, states are faced with the challenge of demonstrating continuous improvement in student performance in reading and mathematics. Attaining goals that are defined by benchmark and subsequent levels of performance and then factored into a school accountability system are critical components of the federal legislation. Beginning in 2007 to 2008, science will be the third content area with required assessments under the NCLB Act. The challenge of interpreting changes in student performance from one grade to the next has been discussed with a greater sense of urgency since the passage of the NCLB Act.

The process of expressing test scores from several successive grades onto a common scale is not new. Almost from the dawn of testing, it has been carried out under the grade equivalent umbrella for many subjects taught in elementary schools. Using the context of the Iowa Tests of Basic Skills (ITBS; Hieronymus & Hoover, 1986), for example, Petersen, Kolen, and Hoover (1989) indicated "the content represented in all levels of a test from an elementary achievement test battery can be viewed as defining a developmental continuum for a particular area of achievement" (p. 231). A developmental scale may therefore be appropriate for this situation. The construction of such a scale requires a statistical process called vertical equating (Slinde & Linn, 1977). More contemporary writers prefer the terms *vertical scaling* or *vertical linking* (Linn & Kiplinger, 1995; National Research Council, 1998).

Many norm-referenced test developers have been successful in constructing developmental scales in the subject areas of reading and mathematics for grade spans such Grades 3 through 8, thanks to the substantial content overlap across grade levels. Unlike reading and mathematics, however, science curriculum and instruction may become more grade-level specific in junior high and high school. Science content at these levels may transition from earth science to physical science, to biology, to chemistry, to physics and beyond, with little overlap in content or a common underlying dimension that would support linking performance across grades or courses.

Mislevy (1992) and Linn (1993) have discussed types of linking methods that seek to add a level of comparability across different assessments. Each author discusses the different levels of comparability in terms of the strength of the link that a given method provides. Practically, the question remains about how to interpret these data in the context of the political questions that need to be answered. As an extension of this linking research, Lissitz and Huynh (2003) reported on a strategy that they described as "vertical moderation" of standards. One example of this is the standard-setting process used for the South Carolina Palmetto Achievement Challenge Tests (PACT) 1999 assessments in English language arts (ELA) and mathematics for Grades 3 though 8. In this approach, standards were set for endpoint grades using a common set of performance-level definitions for the achievement levels and then interpolating achievement-level values for the intermediary grade levels (Huynh, Meyer, & Barton, 2000). Considering these existing options served as the impetus for this study.

In this article, we use a case study approach to describe the method used by the South Carolina Department of Education (SCDE) to set achievement levels for the elementary science assessments that comprise the PACT. We chose to focus on Grades 3 through 6 for this study because the science content in the elementary grade levels may be more coherent than the more course-specific science content that tends to appear beginning in junior high. Note that both South Carolina and the NCLB Act (2001) view Grade 6 as middle school. The NCLB Act has three grade designations—3 through 5, 6 through 9, and 10 through 12.

In the following sections of this article, we describe South Carolina's elementary science assessments and that state's approach to setting achievement levels on those tests. We also provide descriptions for how the state developed a system of vertically moderated standards (VMSs) across the range of grades covered by the tests. Included in that process are standard-setting activities, Technical Advisory Committee (TAC) deliberations, State Department of Education final decisions, and data provided to the state's Board of Education for information purposes. We also provide recommendations for practice.

PACT SCIENCE ASSESSMENTS AND STATE ACCOUNTABILITY SYSTEM

South Carolina's PACT in ELA, mathematics, science, and social studies are part of the state's assessment system and are used to measure students' performance on the state content standards in these areas. All South Carolina public school students in Grades 3 through 8 participate in PACT assessments. Both individual- and school-level provisions are included in the state's accountability system, which uses PACT scores. These provisions are detailed in the S.C. Education Accountability Act of 1998 (South Carolina Code of Laws, 1998). In summary, students who perform below standards are identified for additional assistance and participate in an academic plan designed to bring them up to the level expected by the standards.

Schools receive two ratings under the state accountability system; one for the percentage of its students meeting standards and one for the level of improvement of its students. South Carolina includes both science and social studies in its state accountability system. Thus, the challenge of articulating students' performance across grade level is current with respect to the state's accountability system and proactive in terms of future NCLB Act (2001) requirements.

The PACT science assessments are intended to provide information on the extent to which students in Grades 3 though 8 have attained knowledge and skills in inquiry, life science, earth science, and physical science. The assessments are based on the curriculum frameworks and content standards approved by the State Board of Education. One objective of administering the PACT science examinations is to classify students into one of four achievement levels: *below basic, basic, proficient,* and *advanced.* The operational test forms were developed by the SCDE in conjunction with a contractor that provided test construction, administration, scoring, and reporting services.

The following performance-level descriptions (PLDs; policy definitions) broadly define the achievement levels into which students in South Carolina are classified on the PACT science assessments. They are similar to those used for the 1999 PACT assessments in ELA and mathematics (Huynh et al., 2000, p. 38).

Below Basic
This student has not met expectations for student performance based on the curriculum standards approved by the State Board of Education.

Basic
This student has met minimum expectations for student performance based on the curriculum standards approved by the State Board of Education.

Proficient
This student has met expectations for student performance based on the curriculum standards approved by the State Board of Education—this performance level represents the long-term goal for student performance in South Carolina.

Advanced
This student has exceeded expectations based on the curriculum standards approved by the State Board of Education.

The PACT science assessments include a combination of multiple-choice and constructed-response items that assess the specified strands of the science curriculum. All multiple-choice items are scored dichotomously. Each constructed-response item is scored on a 2-, 3-, or 4-point scale based on a rubric developed by SCDE. Table 1 lists the distribution of items and point values by strand.

OVERVIEW OF STANDARD-SETTING METHOD

The recommended range of cut scores that distinguish achievement levels was based on a variation of the bookmark method (Lewis, Mitzel, & Green, 1996; Mitzel, Lewis, Patz, & Green, 2001). This method uses expert judges to examine items on the test and to estimate how a typical student on the border between two levels of proficiency will likely perform on each item. Items are sequenced from

TABLE 1
Science: 2003 PACT Distribution of Point Values by Strand

Grade	Measure	Inquiry Process	Life Sciences	Earth	Physical Science	Total
3	Percentage	39	26	16	18	100
	Multiple-choice points	15	8	6	7	36
	Constructed-response points	0	2	0	0	2
4	Percentage	41	18	23	18	100
	Multiple-choice points	16	8	8	8	40
	Constructed-response points	2	0	2	0	4
5	Percentage	40	24	18	18	100
	Multiple-choice points	16	8	8	8	40
	Constructed-response points	2	3	0	0	5
6	Percentage	42	18	9	32	100
	Multiple-choice points	20	10	5	15	50
	Constructed-response points	4	0	0	3	7

Note. Strand percentages may not total 100 percent due to rounding. From *Technical Documentation for the 2003 Palmetto Achievement Challenge Tests of English Language Arts, Mathematics, Science, and Social Studies* (p. 14) by the South Carolina Department of Education, 2004. Columbia, SC.

least difficult to most difficult and compiled into an ordered-item booklet (OIB). For PACT 2003 standard settings for science, item difficulties used to order the items were estimated from the field and operational test administrations using a one-parameter (Rasch) model for multiple-choice items and a one-parameter (Rasch) partial credit model for constructed response items. In this application, the location of multiple-choice items in the OIB was determined by the point where students had a 0.67 probability of success on the item (Huynh, 1998; Mitzel et al., 2001). The location of each constructed-response item score point was determined by identifying the point at which the upper cumulative probability of achieving that score point or higher was 0.67. Over 50,000 student responses were used to establish item difficulty values.

In general, the bookmark standard-setting process begins with participants working to establish a common description of target examinees (i.e., those who are barely in a level) based on each performance-level description. Using the PLDs as reference points, each participant starts with the easiest item and moves through the OIB until the participant identifies the place where the barely basic student would likely (i.e., with at least a 0.67 probability) answer items up to that point correctly. When the participant places a bookmark at that point, he or she is distinguishing between below basic and basic achievement level. This process is repeated for each achievement level required.

Standard-setting facilitators then lead a discussion of the participants' rationale for their initial bookmark placements relative to the PLDs and the discussion of the target students at each achievement level. This discussion focuses on the content represented by the item and how it reflected the likely performance of the target student. Participants are then provided feedback in terms of the panel's median bookmark placement, the range of placements, and the impact of the median placement based on cumulative performance data.

After seeing impact data and having a discussion of how to interpret it, participants make their second-round bookmark placements. Final cut score recommendations are based on the second-round bookmark placements. A given cut score is determined for each participant by translating the OIB page number into the corresponding theta location and finding the median values of theta across the participants.

THE STANDARD-SETTING WORKSHOPS

The standard-setting workshops for PACT science were conducted in Columbia, South Carolina, July 28 to 29, 2003 for soliciting recommendations from a statewide group of participants outside the SCDE.

Participants were grouped into grade-level teams—third and fourth grade, and fifth and sixth grade, with an equivalent number of educators from each grade level on the team. Each panel provided judgments on both grade-level assessments. The rationale for having educators from both grades represented on the team was to facilitate the articulation of standards across the grade levels. The workshops for setting cut scores used panels of 16 and 15 for the third- and fourth grade teams and the fifth- and sixth-grade teams, respectively. Jaeger (1991) and Raymond and Reid (2001) have suggested that this number of participants may be acceptable for a standard-setting study. The 31 educators across the two panels had an average experience of 17.7 (median = 20.0) years at grade level and content area. These panels were selected and recruited by the SCDE to ensure representation based on geographic location, gender, ethnicity, and district's socioeconomic characteristics.

The standard-setting workshop began for both panels with an introduction that included the purpose of the workshops, the role of the facilitators, an overview of the bookmark method and the standard-setting process, and the goals of the workshops. After this initial orientation to the process, the two panels broke into their grade-level teams.

PLDs

For each panel, facilitators began by presenting the PLDs to the participants and reviewing the standard-setting process. Each of the panels was then further subdivided into smaller groups of 4 to 5 participants in separate areas of the meeting room for an initial discussion of the knowledge, skills, and abilities of target students. Participants discussed the distinctions that differentiated students' performance for each of the four achievement levels. Using input from these smaller groups, the entire panel established a consolidated understanding of the distinctions between below basic and basic, basic and proficient, and proficient and advanced performances. These discussions were transcribed, printed, and copies distributed to participants so that they could refer to them during their operational judgments. This discussion occurred separately for each respective grade level's standard-setting judgments.

Practice Activities

After discussing the PLDs and distinctions among levels, participants engaged in a practice activity that allowed them to use a practice set of items to place the bookmarks that separated the four achievement levels. Participants repeated the bookmark placement process for each of the three cut points—below basic and basic, basic and proficient, and proficient and advanced. By placing their bookmark in a given location, participants were judging that the items before each bookmark represented content that students at that achievement level have a high probability (at least 0.67) of answering correctly. For constructed-response items, the bookmark indicated that the target student was likely to obtain the score point indicated on items placed before the bookmark. The participants discussed the median and range of bookmark pages established by the panel, anchoring their discussion to the PLDs and achievement-level distinctions elicited in the group's earlier discussions. The participants were also shown impact data reflecting the approximate percentage of previous test takers who would have been classified at each achievement level when using the group's initial median bookmark placement. Participants then took their respective grade-level assessment without the answer key. This exposed participants to the range of content and item difficulty found in the item bank.

First Rounds of Bookmarks

Following this activity, participants engaged in the first round of bookmark placements using the operational OIBs. After round one, feedback data were provided to the participants in terms of median page placement for each panel's respective cut point, range of page placements, discussion of bookmark placements, and impact associated with the median page placement. The discussion of the bookmark placements focused on the content represented by the items around the panel's initial recommended bookmark placement (median), at the higher end of the range of initial recommendations, and at the lower end of the range of initial recommendations. Participants were asked to characterize their bookmark placements with respect to the content represented by the bookmark relative to the PLDs that had been discussed and transcribed for the participants earlier. These discussions often reflected educators' experiences with their students who had skills represented by the various achievement levels defined by the performance-level descriptors.

Second Round of Bookmarks

After seeing these data and discussing the content that was represented by their initial recommended bookmark placement, participants were asked to make a second bookmark placement. The second-round placement could be either the same or different from the participant's initial bookmark. The eventual cut score is based on the second bookmark placement and is determined, for each participant, by translating the OIB page number into the corresponding theta location and then calculating the median value across the participants. The panel's second-round median bookmark placement served as the starting point for all participants for the subsequent bookmark placement. Specifically, the basic and proficient bookmark could not be placed before the group's second-round recommendation for the below basic and basic bookmark. This process iterated sequentially from the lowest bookmark placement to the highest bookmark placement.

Workshop Evaluation

The final activity for the participants was the completion of an evaluation form designed to measure the level of comfort and confidence in the judgments about the cut-score recommendations. After finishing their item ratings, student classifications, and evaluation forms, materials were collected. After the evaluations were completed, each participant was provided with a certificate of participation and the respective workshop was concluded.

In general, the participants were positive about the experience and their involvement in the standard-setting workshop. Some participants offered suggestions for future studies. Two participants requested copies of the content standards for each grade level on which they were setting cut scores. One participant indicated that there should have been more time to discuss specific items in the assessment, and another participant requested that future workshops include a suggestion sheet for them to comment on specific items.

Results

In Round 1, participants provided their initial recommended achievement levels before being given actual performance data. The Round 1 recommended cut scores, standard errors (*SEs*), and the percentages of students at or above each cut score are shown in Table 2.

TABLE 2
Round 1 Recommended Cut Scores, Standard Errors (SE), and
Percentage of Students Scoring At or Above Each Cut Score

| | Basic Cut Score | | | Proficient Cut Score | | | Advanced Cut Score | | |
Grade	Mdn	SE	% At or Above	Mdn	SE	% At or Above	Mdn	SE	% At or Above
3	−1.99	.52	99.6	.76	.41	23.2	1.99	.48	2.0
4	−.55	.35	81.4	.49	.34	30.8	1.58	.40	4.6
5	−.49	.41	74.6	.57	.35	21.4	1.28	.37	4.1
6	−.30	.57	76.4	.29	.31	43.0	1.19	.34	6.6

Note. *Mdn* = median.

Medians and *SE*s shown in Table 2 are reported on the theta scale metric. The *SE*s reported were a combined measure that included the sampling *SE*s of the participants' median judgments and the conditional *SE*s computed at the cut score using the Rasch item difficulty estimates. As indicated in Huynh (2003), these were calculated using $[SE(\text{median})^2 + SEM^2]^{1/2}$, where SE(median) is the SE of the median of the participants' judgments and SEM is the standard error of measurement of the recommended theta value. Under normality, the SE of the median equals 1.25 times the traditional SE of the mean.

The participants' final recommended achievement levels were based on their Round 2 bookmark placements. These placements were made after receiving the performance data described previously. The Round 2 recommended cut scores and other statistics are shown in Table 3.

The impact of the basic cut score ranged from approximately 75% to 90% of students being classified at or above basic across grade levels. The impact of the

TABLE 3
Round 2 Recommended Cut Scores, Standard Errors (SE), and
Percentage of Students Scoring At or Above Each Cut Score

| | Basic Cut Score | | | Proficient Cut Score | | | Advanced Cut Score | | |
Grade	Mdn	SE	% At or Above	Mdn	SE	% At or Above	Mdn	SE	% At or Above
3	−.97	.42	89.9	.85	.37	18.9	1.62	.42	4.6
4	−.70	.35	85.3	.75	.34	21.9	1.61	.41	4.6
5	−.49	.39	74.6	.61	.34	21.4	1.22	.36	4.1
6	−.46	.31	80.2	.29	.30	43.0[a]	1.12	.33	6.6
Average			80.2			20.7			5.0

Note. *Mdn* = median.
[a]Not used in computing the average.

proficient cut score ranged from approximately 19% to 43% across grade levels. The Grade 6 results were at the high end of the range for the proficient cut score. Because the panels that recommended these cut scores were grouped into a third- and fourth-grade team and a fifth- and sixth-grade team, it might be hypothesized that the impact across the grades covered by a grade-level team would be similar. Although this phenomenon was evident for the third and fourth grade, it was not observed in the fifth- and sixth-grade panel. The impact of the advanced cut score ranged from approximately 4% to 7% across grade levels. Again, there was less variability in recommended cut scores observed for the third- and fourth-grade panel than was observed in the fifth- and sixth-grade panel. The Round 2 results were taken as the cut scores recommended by the participants in the standard-setting workshop.

TAC REVIEW AND SCDE DELIBERATIONS

On July 8 and 9, 2003, data were presented to members of the TAC and SCDE in Columbia, South Carolina. At this meeting, the standard-setting contractor described the standard-setting procedures and presented the results of the workshops. Specifically these results were the median panel-recommended cut scores distinguishing each achievement level, a range of values for each cut score identifying ±1, ±2, and ±3 SEs, impact data in terms of the percentage of students at or above each cut score, and the results of the workshop evaluations.

The TAC agreed that the final cut scores should result in impact that is relatively stable across grade levels, displays an across-grade trend line that is similar to other PACT assessments, is consistent with PACT results in mathematics, and is supported by national and state data from sources such as the National Assessment Educational Progress (NAEP) science results and the previous state assessment in science. Finally, the TAC advised that adjustments, if any, to the recommended cut scores should be made within the range of two standard errors of the judgments from the bookmark standard-setting process.

Pertinent to SCDE deliberations are the data of Tables 4 and 5. Table 4 provides the range of impact data (i.e., percentage of students at or above each cut score) defined at the end point of the participant-recommended cut scores plus or minus 1 to 3 SEs.

Table 5 provides a summary of the external data from three sources (a) NAEP; (b) the previous state assessment program (the Basic Skills Assessment Program [BSAP]; SCDE, 1998); and (c) PACT data.

The SCDE technical staff carefully examined the overall nature of the impact data associated with each cut score recommended by the participants. Excluding the proficient cut score for Grade 5, the impact data appeared relatively consistent

TABLE 4
Range of the Percentage of Students Scoring At or Above Each Cut Score

Grade	Interval	% At or Above Basic Cut-Score Range	% At or Above Proficient Cut-Score Range	% At or Above Advanced Cut-Score Range
3	PRC ± 1 SE	75 to 96	9 to 33	2 to 9
	PRC ± 2 SEs	56 to 99.1	5 to 44	0.6 to 19
	PRC ± 3 SEs	38 to 99.6	2 to 62	0.3 to 33
4	PRC ± 1 SE	72 to 94	11 to 36	1 to 9
	PRC ± 2 SEs	57 to 97	7 to 52	0.4 to 22
	PRC ± 3 SEs	41 to 99	3 to 68	0.2 to 36
5	PRC ± 1 SE	58 to 87	11 to 36	2 to 11
	PRC ± 2 SEs	36 to 96	4 to 52	0.3 to 26
	PRC ± 3 SEs	17 to 99	2 to 69	0.2 to 41
6	PRC ± 1 SE	68 to 92	24 to 58	3 to 13
	PRC ± 2 SEs	48 to 97	13 to 76	0.8 to 28
	PRC ± 3 SEs	33 to 99	7 to 87	0.3 to 43

Note. PRC = Participant recommended cut score. SE = standard error.

TABLE 5
Summary of External Data Considered by the Technical Advisory Committee

Assessment	% At or Above Basic	% At or Above Proficient	% At or Above Advanced
NAEP Science 1996 Grade 4	67	29	3
NAEP Science 1996 Grade 8	61	29	4
NAEP Science 2000 Grade 4	66	29	4
NAEP Science 2000 Grade 8	61	32	4
Average	64	30	4
PACT Math 1999 Grade 3	56	18	5.3
PACT Math 1999 Grade 4	55	17	4.6
PACT Math 1999 Grade 5	53	16	4.4
PACT Math 1999 Grade 6	53	16	4.5
Average	54	17	4.7
BSAP Science 1998 Grade 3	64		
BSAP Science 1998 Grade 6	52		
BSAP Science 1998 Grade 8	44		
Average	53		
Overall Average	57	23	4.2

Note. NAEP = National Assessment Educational Progress; PACT = South Carolina Palmetto Achievement Challenge Tests; BSAP = Basic Skills Assessment Program. For the BSAP, these are the percentages of passing students.

across all grade levels. The percentage of students at or above the cut score stood at 82% for basic, 21% for proficient, and 5% for advanced.

The SCDE staff first considered the basic cut score. Considering the fact that the PACT science assessments were at a fairly new stage, the staff judged that the percentage of 82% for students at basic or above was too high. Indeed, this percentage was much higher than similar data from external sources. As stated, these sources were the PACT mathematics assessment at the same stage in 1999 (54%), the NAEP science tests (65%), and the BSAP science tests (53%). The percentage of 82% was also judged as inconsistent with the instructional purposes of the PACT assessments, which aim in part at identifying students who would need instructional help. Finally, for the basic cut score, the staff noted that the average of the external data was at about 57%. Following the TAC recommendation, the staff arrived at the tentative basic cut scores that were within the 2-SE bands and about 57%. As in the case of the PACT 1999 assessments in ELA and mathematics assessment, a linear trend line was used on the impact data to arrive at all cut scores (Huynh et al., 2000).

At the proficient cut score, the SCDE noted that there is considerable overall agreement in the percentage of students at proficient and above between the participants (21%) and the average external data from PACT mathematics and NAEP. Excluding Grade 6, the staff recommended cut scores in the range recommended by the participants. A linear trend line based on Grades 3 to 5 was used to arrive at the Grade 6 cut score.

The tentative cut scores derived by the SCDE staff were relayed to the TAC for comments and suggestions. Upon acceptance from the State Superintendent of Education, the cut scores established by the SCDE staff were then taken as the final cut scores for the PACT science assessments and presented to the State Board of Education for information.

Table 6 presents the impact data of the cut scores that were adopted by the SCDE.

TABLE 6
Impact Data for Cut Scores Adopted for PACT Science Assessments

Grade	% At or Above Basic	% At or Above Proficient	% At or Above Advanced
3	56.2	23.2	6.5
4	57.1	21.9	6.5
5	58.2	21.4	7.9
6	58.4	20.1	6.6
Average	57.4	21.7	6.9

Note. PACT = South Carolina Palmetto Achievement Challenge Tests.

The report to the Board (SCDE, 2003) included the following points regarding the SCDE decision on the official cut score for the PACT 2003 science assessments.

1. Participants were informed that their role in the process was advisory and that the TAC would review their recommendations with a final decision being made by the department.
2. The TAC reviewed the panel's recommendations and observed inconsistencies across grade levels. The following considerations were suggested and employed in determining the cut scores:
   - Cut scores should result in relatively consistent results across grade levels within a subject.
   - Science results should be more closely related to mathematics results.
   - Score patterns should be supported by external data, including PACT math results from 1999, NAEP science results in Grades 4 and 8 from 1996 and 2000, and BSAP science results from Grades 3, 6, and 8 from 1998. The proposed cut scores tend to follow the patterns of NAEP (although the NAEP standards appeared to be generally more demanding) and BSAP (although the BSAP standards appeared to be generally less demanding).
3. Although the committees were not always consistent, cut scores should fall within a 2-*SE* band around the panels' recommendation whenever feasible.

DISCUSSION

Although informed by judgmental strategies, the ultimate outcome of standard-setting activities remains a policy decision that needs to support the purpose of the assessment system. If assessment systems are intended to be complementary, then the results of these systems should convey the uniqueness of each system's purpose. Systems that cannot be distinguished from one another may reflect redundancy in the assessment systems that can be revised for greater efficiency. Communicating the connections among the elements in an assessment system requires an understanding of how the pieces fit together (Cizek, 1995). It appears simplistic to suggest that the results for the program at the heart of this study should fall somewhere between a more stringent program (i.e., NAEP) and a less stringent program (i.e., BSAP). Many may also question why a standard-setting study was even needed for the PACT assessment in this study if the upper and lower boundaries of expected student performance were already defined a priori. To communicate a meaningful relation among these assessments in the broader system, the policy decision needed to consider these additional sources of information. Although the policy question may be addressed, the psychometric questions linger.

From a measurement perspective, when judgments from standard-setting methods fall within an expected range relative to other assessments of similar content, it provides confirmatory validity evidence for the procedure. We know that different tests have different purposes and different definitions of performance. Thus, the results from these should represent each test's contribution to the assessment system as a whole. Second, conducting standard-setting studies, alignment, and opportunity to learn studies provides information about whether there is a coherent curriculum and consistent instruction across grade levels. We could speculate that some of the variation in the results across grade levels observed in this study might be explained by differences in curricular content and emphasis in science. Third, these activities allow programs to examine whether or not the characteristic develops across grade levels. In this application, there was an attempt to vertically moderate standards in a content area for which it may or may not be conducive. Because of greater course specificity beginning in Grade 7, we chose to focus on the Grade 3 through 6 science assessments, expecting there to be greater coherence across those grade levels.

An additional measurement question that needs to be explored relates to the challenge of setting multiple cut scores for an assessment. This question revolves around the extent of the inferences that can be drawn from an assessment and could be characterized as opportunities to demonstrate performance. If there are limited measurement opportunities at each desired level of inference (e.g., below basic, basic, proficient, advanced), there will likely be greater fluctuation in the cut scores that are recommended by the panel, making moderation across grade levels more tenuous (Buckendahl, 2004; Ryan, 2004). Because other states and assessment systems are also faced with this challenge, we offer three recommendations for practice:

1. Utilize relevant, additional data sources to guide the final policy decision-making process and add greater consistency to the complementary tests that may be in place in the broader assessment system.

2. Operationally define performance across grade levels a priori to support the desired articulation in the recommended performance standards. Anchoring performance-level decisions in the content provides greater support for the policy descriptions and demonstrates to stakeholders the types of knowledge, skills, and abilities that may be observed at a given performance level.

3. Evaluate inconsistencies in recommended performance standards for evidence that may not support the policy decisions. For example, if one grade level demonstrates a large discrepancy in the recommended performance standard from what was expected given corollary information, there may be curricular, instructional, and/or assessment explanations for the difference that need to be addressed.

CONCLUSION

The challenge of setting standards that consider the characteristics of the target student and consider the difficulty of the assessment, yet meaningfully articulate across grade levels is nontrivial. In trying to demonstrate growth in a content area for federal accountability purposes, states are faced with balancing the recommendations for performance standards with the policies that flow from them. As we described in this article, South Carolina did not rely solely on the information gathered from the standard-setting workshops for the PACT Science Assessments, but included additional assessment information to guide the ultimate policy recommendation. By considering assessment systems that are designed for different purposes in the decision-making process, it allows for greater consistency among the systems.

ACKNOWLEDGMENT

We acknowledge the support of the South Carolina Department of Education in this project. We also are grateful for the feedback provided by Greg Cizek on an earlier version of this article.

REFERENCES

Buckendahl, C. W. (2004, June). *Evaluating sufficiency of measurement in state assessment programs.* Paper presented at the National Conference on Large Scale Assessment, Boston, MA.

Cizek, G. J. (1995). The big picture in assessment and who ought to have it. *Phi Delta Kappan, 77,* 246–249.

Hieronymus, A. N., & Hoover, H. D. (1986). *Iowa Tests of Basic Skills manual for school administrators.* Chicago: Riverside.

Huynh, H. (1998). On score locations of binary and partial credit items and their applications to item mapping and criterion-referenced interpretation. *Journal of Educational and Behavioral Statistics, 23,* 35–56.

Huynh, H. (2003, August). *Technical memorandum for computing standard error in bookmark standard-setting.* (The South Carolina PACT 2003 Standard Setting Support Project). Columbia: University of South Carolina.

Huynh, H., Meyer, P., & Barton, K. (2000, October). *Technical documentation for the South Carolina PACT–1999 Tests.* Columbia: South Carolina Department of Education. Retrieved March 27, 2004 from http://www.myscschools.com

Jaeger, R. M. (1991). Selection of judges for standard-setting. *Educational Measurement: Issues and Practices, 10*(2), 3–6, 10, 14.

Lewis, D. M., Mitzel, H. C., & Green, D. R. (1996, June). *Standard setting: A bookmark approach.* Paper presented at the National Conference on Large-Scale Assessment, Phoenix, AZ.

Linn, R. L. (1993). Linking results of distinct assessments. *Applied Measurement in Education, 6*, 83–102.

Linn, R. L., & Kiplinger, V. L. (1995). Linking statewide tests to the National Assessment of Educational Progress: Stability of results. *Applied Measurement in Education, 8*, 135–155.

Lissitz, R. W., & Huynh, H. (2003). Vertical equating for state assessments: Issues and solutions in determination of adequate yearly progress and school accountability. *Practical Assessment, Research & Evaluation, 8*(10). Retrieved May 8, 2003 from http://ericae.net/pare/getvn.asp?v=8&n=10

Mislevy, R. J. (1992). *Linking educational assessments: Concepts, issues, methods, and prospects.* Princeton, NJ: Educational Testing Service.

Mitzel, H. C., Lewis, D. M., Patz, R. J., & Green, D. R. (2001). The bookmark method: Psychological perspectives. In G. J. Cizek (Ed.) *Setting performance standards: Concepts, methods, and perspectives* (pp. 249–281). Mahwah, NJ: Lawrence Erlbaum Associates, Inc.

National Center for Education Statistics (2001, November). *National science achievement-level results, Grades 4 and 8: 1996 and 2000.* Retrieved March 1, 2004, from http://nces.ed.gov/nationreportcard/science/results

National Research Council. (1998). *Uncommon measures: Equivalence and linkage among educational tests.* Washington, DC: National Academy Press.

No Child Left Behind Act of 2001, Pub. L. No. 107–110, 115 Stat.1425 (2002).

Petersen, N. S., Kolen, M. J., & Hoover, H. D. (1988). Scaling, norming, and equating. In R. L. Linn (Ed.), *Educational measurement* (3rd ed., pp. 221–262). New York: Macmillan.

Raymond, M. R., & Reid, J. B. (2001). Who made thee a judge? Selecting and training participants for standard-setting. In G. J. Cizek (Ed.) *Setting performance standards: Concepts, methods, and perspectives* (pp. 119–157). Mahwah, NJ: Lawrence Erlbaum & Associates, Inc.

Ryan, J. M. (2004, June). *Can state assessment programs classify students and provide useful interpretations of students' achievement?* Paper presented at the National Conference on Large Scale Assessment, Boston, MA.

Slinde, J. A., & Linn, R. L. (1977). Vertically equate tests: Fact or phantom? *Journal of Educational Measurement, 14*, 23–32.

South Carolina Code of Laws. (1998). *S.C. Education Accountability Act of 1998.* Retrieved February 2, 2004 from http://www.myscschools.com/archive/ednews/1998/98accact.htm

South Carolina Department of Education. (1998). *BSAP: 1998 Results of the Basic Skills Assessment Program.* Retrieved March 1, 2004, from http://www.myscschools.com/reports/BSAP/bsapdata.htm

South Carolina Department of Education. (2003). Report presented to the State Board of Education, August 27. Columbia, SC: Author.

South Carolina Department of Education. (2004). *Technical documentation for the 2003 Palmetto Achievement Challenge Tests of english language arts, mathematics, science, and social studies.* Columbia, SC: Authors

APPLIED MEASUREMENT IN EDUCATION, *18*(1), 99–113

Vertically Moderated Standards: Background, Assumptions, and Practices

Huynh Huynh and Christina Schneider

College of Education
University of South Carolina

Developmental (vertical) scales are often constructed for subject areas such as reading and mathematics that are taught continuously in elementary schools. In other subjects such as science, and across a wider grade span, such scales are hard to justify. For tracking student progress and school accountability (including the No Child Left Behind Act of 2001) purposes, it may be more feasible to rely on a system of vertically moderated standards (VMS). The purpose of this article is to (a) describe VMS, (b) present the assumptions that underline VMS, and (c) review the steps the National Assessment of Educational Progress took in regard to the decision to decrease reliance on across-grade scaling in a number of subject areas.

Across the years, many assessment programs have been designed to measure students' achievement in a specified subject area and to track their progress across several grade levels. One example is the case of the Iowa Tests of Basic Skills (ITBS; Hieronymus & Hoover, 1986). Within the ITBS context, Petersen, Kolen, and Hoover (1989) indicated that "the content represented in all levels of a test from an elementary achievement test battery can be viewed as defining a *developmental continuum* [italics added] for a particular area of achievement" (p. 231). A developmental scale may therefore be appropriate for this situation. The construction of such a scale requires a statistical process called "vertical equating" (Slinde & Linn, 1977). Many contemporary writers prefer the term *vertical scaling* or *vertical linking*. Wherever appropriate, vertical scales have proven to be helpful in assessing the growth of individual students from one year to the next.

The No Child Left Behind (NCLB) Act (2001) and state school accountability legislation such as the South Carolina Education Accountability Act of 1998

Requests for reprints should be sent to Huynh Huynh, College of Education, University of South Carolina, Columbia, SC 29208. E-mail: huynh-huynh@sc.edu

(South Carolina Code of Laws, 1998) have increased states' needs to track student progress across grade levels in two main areas. First, states are now required to administer annual reading and mathematics assessments to students in Grades 3 through 8 (science is to be implemented soon), along with a high school examination that is administered over content covered in Grades 10 through 12. Second, states are required to determine if students within schools achieve adequate yearly progress (AYP). The NCLB Act stipulated that states must hold all students within each elementary school and secondary school to the same level of achievement in regard to state standards. Essential components of AYP that relate to VMS are that the progress of schools and districts must be measured on assessments based on state standards, and the achievement of students has to be disaggregated into the following subgroups: (a) economically disadvantaged, (b) major racial and ethnic groups, (c) students with disabilities, and (d) students with limited English proficiency. For schools and districts to successfully meet AYP targets, each subgroup population within a school must reach a state-specified target in regard to the percentage of students at or above the state-defined proficient level. Schools, in particular Title I schools, that fail to achieve AYP for multiple consecutive years face serious sanctions.

A vertical scale may facilitate school accountability and NCLB (2001) obligations in some situations. Aside from subject areas such as reading and mathematics, which are taught continuously across the elementary grades, such a scale may be difficult to construct in subject areas like science or social studies. Beyond the first few grades, content coverage in these areas tends to concentrate on grade-specific strands and therefore makes across-grade linking a challenging task. In an attempt to construct a vertical scale for the science tests for one state, for example, D. Thissen (personal communication, July 21, 2004) wrote that

> Because entirely different "topics" were taught in each grade, the scale showed no increase across grades (as one would reasonably expect). Fifth graders scored no higher on the fourth-grade test than did fourth graders (because the fifth graders had not been taught any more fourth grade science; they were taught something else). A "flat" scale is useless and was abandoned.

Thissen also added that "this depends on the curriculum, of course. One would imagine a developmentally integrated curriculum that would show growth across grades." To facilitate vertical scaling in science and social studies, the Illinois Assessment Framework (IAF; Illinois State Board of Education, 2003), for example, included the following requirement:

> "In Science the IAF expectations at Grade 7 include the content addressed at Grade 4. Likewise, in Social Science the IAF expectations at Grade 8 include the content addressed at Grade 5. Thus, while the assessment objectives from the specified grade

will comprise the bulk of the tests in any given year, content from earlier grade levels is also eligible for state assessment. (p. 2)

It is not known how many large-scale assessment programs require an across-grade accumulation of content in designing the test at each grade level.

Rather than attempting the construction of a vertical when the conditions are somewhat strenuous, Lissitz and Huynh (2003) argued for a system of vertically moderated standards (VMS). The VMS concept is not new and has been used in large-scale assessment programs like the South Carolina Palmetto Achievement Challenge Tests (PACT; Huynh, Meyer, & Barton, 2000).

In this article, we have three major purposes: (a) to review the steps the National Assessment of Educational Progress (NAEP) took in regard to the decision to decrease reliance on across-grade scaling in a number of subject areas, (b) to describe VMS and the assumptions that underline VMS, and (c) to describe a number of situations where VMS might be useful. First, however, we will provide some detailed background on vertical scaling.

VERTICAL SCALING

In addition to the ITBS cited previously, vertical scales have been constructed for other standardized tests such as the TerraNova (CTB/McGraw-Hill, 1997, 2001) and the Stanford Achievement Test (Harcourt Educational Measurement, 2003, 2004). State assessment programs with vertical scales for reading and mathematics include Mississippi (Tomkowicz & Schaeffer, 2002) and Colorado (Colorado Department of Education, 2003).

The major assumption required for the creation of a vertical scale is that of unidimensionality for the trait being measured. For any educational achievement test, it has been argued that the subject matter must also be highly homogeneous and that the cognitive dimensions are similar at each subsequent grade level. This assumption of unidimensionality of homogenous test content may be considered more easily satisfied when a vertical scale is constructed for two adjacent grades and in content areas such as reading or mathematics, though in this case, it is often argued that a vertical scale may not capture the grade-specific dimensions that may be of considerable importance. For example, in reading, changes in content may lead to a different focus in instruction. Initial instruction may focus on reading fluency, move to comprehension, and then begin to focus on conclusions and inferences. This is evident in the current frameworks for reading used by NAEP that specify three different contexts in which reading should be measured: reading to perform a task, reading for information, and reading for literary experience. At Grade 4, however, only two reading contexts are measured: reading for information and reading for literary experience (National Assessment Governing Board [NAGB], 2002).

To exacerbate the issue of content focus, oftentimes, in the areas of science and social studies, the dimensions or content areas change dramatically from year to year. The two assumptions of unidimensionality and homogenous content assessed across time may not be tenable. For this reason, it may not be reasonable to construct a vertical scale for subject areas such as these.

ACROSS-GRADE AND WITHIN-GRADE SCALING ON NAEP

Over many years, NAEP has served as a model of psychometric quality and innovation. Many state assessment programs have mirrored the procedures used by NAEP in the creation of assessment frameworks, the composition of test forms, item writing, item analysis and calibration, and test score reporting and interpretation. For the NAEP assessments, a major aspect of test score interpretation is embodied in scaling and achievement level (AL) setting. Although tests such as the TerraNova and the Stanford Achievement Test (SAT) continue to report test scores using vertical (i.e., across-grade, developmental) scales, NAEP has abandoned its earlier practice of across-grade scaling for new assessments. In this section of the article, we review some of the rationales behind this rethinking of the utility of a vertical scale.

Over several cycles, NAEP reported on student achievement in Grades 4, 8, and 12 in reading and mathematics using across-grade scales. In the early 1990s, new efforts were devoted to improving the way NAEP reported (Bock 1991; E. Elliott, personal communication to J. Finn, April 23, 1991; E. Haertel, personal communication to R. Truby, January 8, 1990; E. Haertel, personal communication to L. Bourque, May 9, 1990). Based on the recommendation of the NAEP Technical Review Panel, in 1991, the NAGB adopted the position that in future assessments, when possible, NAEP would report scores on a within-grade scale rather than on an across-grade or vertical scale.

This position was adopted based upon the controversy regarding the across-grade scale surrounding the NAEP 1990 Mathematics Assessment (Haertel, 1991). Haertel noted that the mix of content and process categories represented in the different areas of the vertically equated scale were likely to differ, and he cited this as one reason psychometricians were not supportive of the vertical scale. This scaling issue is, in essence, a validity issue because NAEP frameworks often specify different content and process category allocations by grade level.

Haertel (1991) provided a second reason to approach vertical scales with caution. He noted that vertical scales have the potential for ceiling and floor effects. Cook and Campbell (1979) defined ceiling effects when an assessment is not sensitive enough to measure the gain that may occur within one group, and they defined floor effects as occurring when scores from a particular group cluster at the bottom end of a scale. Through the use of a vertical scale, Haertel noted the potential for administering items that are too difficult for young students (therefore, scores may cluster in the low end of a scale) and too easy for older students (therefore, true gain may not be measured). In such cases, precise measures of student abilities at particular points along the scale would not be obtained. Finally, Haertel noted that comparison of subgroup differences across grade levels likely revolves around whether these differences are getting larger or smaller over time. This interpretation is especially of interest in the AYP environment, yet as Haertel observed, the interpretation may not appropriate because grade levels may not be equally distanced on the vertical scale.

Although NAEP continues to report reading and mathematics on the across-grade scales (for reasons of continuity in trend reports), other areas, such as science and writing, are reported using within-grade scales. Changes in the reading and mathematics scales, however, are slowly occurring. First, although current results are always linked back to the original scale, NAGB has discontinued the development of across-grade items. Second, because the NAEP 12th Grade mathematics test framework for 2005 has changed substantially from previous years, new ALs are being set (NAGB, 2003). Additionally, because of the more rigorous algebra and geometry content on the 2005 Grade-12 NAEP (as compared with other grade levels), the across-grade scale will be broken for Grade 12.

NAEP STANDARD-SETTING PROCEDURES AND RESULTS FOR GRADES 4, 8, AND 12 IN READING, MATHEMATICS, AND SCIENCE

A system of VMS involves several performance categories. Although pass–fail (binary) classifications have been used over the years in many state assessment programs to classify students on tests measuring basic competency, current practice relies more on three or more categories.

The NAEP has used a system of ALs to describe what students should know and be able to do in subject areas including reading, mathematics, and science. The NAGB—the policy-making panel for NAEP—was authorized by Congress to set achievement goals for student performance on the NAEP. The NAGB made the decision in 1990 to use three ALs (named *basic*, *proficient*, and *advanced*) to describe student achievement. The NAGB considered a multitude of technical and political factors in making its decisions on the ALs such as those in the NAEP science assessments (M.L. Bourque, personal communication, May 2004). Those ALs were implemented in 1992 for reading and mathematics, and in 1996 for science in Grades 4, 8, and 12. Details on NAEP methods and practices in AL standard-setting and how they evolved across the years are documented in Loomis and Bourque (2001a).

Four general observations can be made regarding the NAEP ALs setting processes and results:

1. There is a use of set of common policy definitions for the ALs.
2. There is a statistical measure of uncertainty in making adjustments, if any, to participants' initial recommended cut scores.
3. There is the consideration of a variety of related student performance data that are external to NAEP when finalizing NAEP ALs.
4. There is a presence of a monotonic across-grade trend line in the percentage of student in the *below basic* category in the three content areas of reading, mathematics, and science. The following sections of this article, we provide additional detail on these observations.

Use of a Common Set of Policy Definitions

As documented in Loomis and Bourque (2001b; 2001c; 2001d), the NAGB adopted common general policy statements regarding what constitutes basic, proficient, and advanced achievement. The achievement-level policy definitions are listed on the website of National Center for Education Statistics (NCES, 2004), and include the following:

Basic: Partial mastery of prerequisite knowledge and skills that are fundamental for proficient work in each grade.
   Proficient: Solid academic performance for each grade assessed. Students reaching this level have demonstrated competency over challenging subject matter, including subject-matter knowledge, application of such knowledge to real-world situations, and analytical skills appropriate to the subject matter.
   Advanced: Superior performance.

The preceding policy definitions have been used for all grades and in all subject areas. Thus, they provide a common across-grade general interpretation for each AL. In a typical standard-setting procedure for NAEP, an initial task for participants was to develop more detailed and explicit achievement-level descriptors (ALDs) for each AL in the subject area. These ALDs then guided the participants in making recommendations about the cut score for each AL. In the case of the ALs set by standard-setting participants for science, NAGB felt that the ALs were not reasonable because they felt some levels were too stringent while others were too lenient (Loomis & Bourque, 2001d). After NAGB adopted ALs it felt to be more reasonable, the original ALDs no longer matched the final cut scores adopted by NAGB and therefore needed to be adjusted on a post hoc basis to reflect these cut scores (M.L Bourque, personal communication, May 2004). Details about the adjustment process and relevant references may be found in Loomis and Bourque (2001d).

Use of a Statistical Measure of Uncertainty

As is well known, all statistical estimators are subject to sampling error and all test scores to measurement error. Uncertainty measures based on each or a combination of these sources of error can be used to make adjustments in a decision-making process. This type of adjustment was used in some NAGB standard-setting situations. For AL settings for mathematics in 1992, for example, the NAGB

> decided that the mathematics standards were too stringent. They took into account the statistical imprecision in estimating the cutscores from ratings and adjusted the cut scores. The cut scores for all grades and levels were set at one standard error below the original overall composite cut scores computed from panelists' ratings (Loomis & Bourque, 2001b, p. 3).

Use of Relevant External Data

In making the decision to adjust the panelists' recommended cut scores for mathematics in 1992, the NAGB also considered information about student course-taking patterns in mathematics and student performance on other assessments in the same subject area. Perhaps the use of external data is most clearly evident in the 1996 AL setting for NAEP science. According to M. L. Bourque (personal communication, May 17, 2004), "the 1996 science assessment had two unusual characteristics that complicated the AL standard-setting. First, a high percentage of the constructed-response items (>80%) mapped onto the NAEP scale above the observed performance of any examinee. Second, the participants were highly variable in their ratings of the constructed-response items." A mismatch between test items and examinees has been known to create difficulty in bookmark standard-settings. For example, some panelists tend to set low and easy standards when the ordered-item booklet is composed of easy items. Conversely, when the booklet is made of difficult items, recommended standards tend to be on the harsh side. Thus it is likely that a mismatch will create more variations in panelists' judgments.

After considerable debate, the NAGB accepted only the panelists' recommended cut scores for Grade 4 proficient and Grade 12 basic levels. The following excerpt from Loomis and Bourque (2001d) provides a record of the internal debate:

> Before setting the Science Achievement Levels, NAGB reviewed achievement level data from other subjects, the 1997 Advanced Placement results in science for twelfth-grade students, and information about eighth-grade student performance in the

Third Internal Mathematics and Science Study. NAGB concluded that the recommendations based on the work of the achievement levels setting panels were not reasonable. The Governing Board judged that some levels were set too high and some were set too low. NABG analyzed the relationship of cutscores to percentages of students scoring at or above different levels and adopted levels that it judged to be reasonable. (p. 3)

Across-Grade Trend Line

Tables 1 through 3 show the percentage of students in various AL categories for the NAEP assessments in reading, mathematics, and science on the year when standard-setting was conducted. The data are taken from Loomis and Bourque (2001b; 2001c; 2001d). Although NAGB made the final decision on the official cut scores after taking into account a multitude of factors, the data in the second column of these tables reflect a consistent trend for the below basic category across the three grades – a decreasing percentage of students are in the lowest category for reading and mathematics, and an increasing percentage of students are in the lowest category for science.

CHARACTERISTICS OF AND CONDITIONS FOR VMS

Like the NAGB, many state assessment programs have used standard-setting processes that bear the four characteristics previously observed for the NAEP ALs setting. One example is the PACT in English language arts and mathematics for Grades 3 through 8 in 1999 (Huynh et al., 2000) and in science for Grades 3 through 6 in 2003 (Buckendahl, Huynh, Siskind, & Saunders, this issue). In such programs, it is desirable to set standards across grades and subjects so that the resulting system of performance standards is coherent and reasonable.

Lissitz and Huynh (2003) have referred to the resulting standards as a system of VMS. There are two basic elements in VMSs.

1. A set of common policy definitions for the ALs (such as basic, proficient, and advanced) is used for all grades.

2. A consistent trend line is imposed on the percentage of students in important performance categories. One such important category is likely the state-defined proficient category in the AYP environment. For assessment programs with a focus on instructional remediation, an important category may be the below basic category. A consistent trend line may reflect no change, a moderate level of increase, or a moderate level of decrease across the grades.

A system of VMS is essentially a mixture of "policy equating" and "linear statistical adjustment" (Mislevy, 1992). Policy equating refers to the common mean-

TABLE 1
Percentage of Students in the NAEP 1992 Reading Achievement
Categories by Grade Level

Grade	Below Basic	Basic and Above	Proficient and Above	Advanced
4	38	62	29	6
8	31	69	31	7
12	20	80	40	4

Note. NAEP = National Assessment of Educational Progress. From *National Assessment of Education Progress Achievement Levels, 1992–1998 for Reading* (pp. 55–58), by S.C. Loomis and M.L. Bourque, 2001, Washington, DC: National Assessment Governing Board.

TABLE 2
Percentage of Students in the NAEP 1992 Mathematics Achievement
Categories by Grade Level

Grade	Below Basic	Basic and Above	Proficient and Above	Advanced
4	50.1	49.9	12.7	1.2
8	48.2	51.8	15.3	2.0
12	41.9	58.1	11.9	1.4

Note. NAEP = National Assessment of Educational Progress. From *National Assessment of Educational Progress Achievement Levels, 1992–1998 for Mathematics* (pp.32–35), by S.C. Loomis and M.L. Bourque, 2001, Washington, DC: National Assessment Governing Board.

TABLE 3
Percentage of Students in the NAEP 1996 Science Achievement
Categories by Grade Level

Grade	Below Basic	Basic and Above	Proficient and Above	Advanced
4	33	67	29	3
8	39	61	29	3
12	43	57	21	3

Note. NAEP = National Assessment of Educational Progress. From *National Assessment of Educational Progress Achievement Levels, 1992–1998 for Mathematics* (pp.32–35), by S.C. Loomis and M.L. Bourque, 2001, Washington, DC: National Assessment Governing Board.

ing that is given to ALs across grade levels. For example, in South Carolina across Grades 3 through 8, a basic student is one who has just barely met the standards; therefore, the student is minimally prepared for work at the next grade level. A proficient student has met the state's expectation for the standards; therefore, the student is well prepared for work at the next grade level (Huynh et al., 2000). Those policy definitions may be the same or reasonably similar across grade levels. This type of policy consistency would foster a stable assessment system for a state's school accountability system and for the AYP requirements of the NCLB Act (2001).

VMS and Test Equating

Mislevy (1992) and Linn and Baker (1993) defined four types of equating: true equating, calibration, projection, and moderation. True equating has the most stringent assumptions. It requires that the equated scores can be used interchangeably; hence, the tests to be equated must measure the same construct with the same degree of reliability. Horizontal equating for within-grade alternate forms of the same test represents a case of true equating. Calibration relaxes the condition of equal reliability and uses a common scale score system to express scores from different tests that measure the same construct albeit with varying degree of precision. Vertical scaling for across-grade test forms is an example of calibration because the error of measurement for a given examinee varies with the test form. Projection is the process of predicting an examinee's score on one test given his or her performance on another test. In the case of projection, the two tests do not have to measure the same construct; however, they must show some level of statistical relation. Finally, the weakest linking is moderation, which occurs when the two tests are not assumed to be measuring the same construct and no statistical data on a relation are available to support a projection. However, scores that are comparable in some statistical sense are still desired. An illustration is the case where two test scores, one on a Korean mathematics test and the other from an American mathematics test, are equated if they have the same z score (linear equating) or the same percentile rank (equal percentile equating).

Statistical moderation is used for VMSs to achieve some consistency in AL percentages across grades. Such consistency assumes that instructional efforts remain relatively uniform across grade levels, and as a consequence, expectations for student achievement should not fluctuate too much across the grades. Teacher training institutions and teacher certification by state departments of education, for example, are typically provided for a span of grade levels like elementary schools in all subject areas or middle schools in specified subject areas. Hence it would be very hard to argue that these teachers would vary their instructional effort or emphasis across the grades for which they are trained and certified.

There are a variety of ways to implement VMS across grades. For the 1999 South Carolina PACTs of English language arts and mathematics for Grades 3 through 8 (Huynh, Barton, Meyer, Porchea, & Gallant, this issue; Huynh et al., 2000), for example, the bookmark process was used in the standard-setting conference to set cut scores at Grades 3 and 8. To determine the cut scores of the other grade levels, interpolation was used with a focus on the percentage of students within each achievement category. The goal is to have a reasonably consistent proportion of students within each achievement category across the six-grade span. Finally, additional evidence from other data sources may be used to support the reasonableness of the VMS. The standard-setting for the South Carolina 2003 PACT of science and social studies (Bukendahl et al., this issue) provides an illustration of using external data.

Use of VMS in Tracking Student Progress

As may sometimes be seen in the interpretation of NAEP's across-grade scale, stakeholders may mistakenly assume that student growth in education occurs at a constant rate, and therefore, stakeholders may make the assumption that appropriate growth on a vertical scale should be an equal number of points each year. However, this assumption is erroneous for a variety of reasons. First, Lissitz and Huynh (2003) noted that equal growth along a vertical scale across grade levels is hard to justify and that the comparison of a student's growth or of subpopulation growth at different grades may not be appropriate. This is because stakeholders may inaccurately assume that grades are spaced an equal distance apart from one another on a vertical scale.

The issue of assuming equal-interval growth is compounded if stakeholders also assume that cut scores for AL categories are an equal distance apart within and across grades. Stakeholders may not realize that cut scores set across achievement-level categories are also not always equally spaced. This has implications if stakeholders interpret an amount of growth at a particular rate as indicating that the student will either continue to show growth at the same rate, or if they believe a student will move from one achievement category to the next based on the previous grade-level growth rate and achievement-level category classification.

To progress across subsequent achievement-level categories, students may be required to grow a greater distance on the vertical scale in some achievement categories and less distance in others within a subject area. Moreover, the growth needed to move across achievement-level categories will likely differ across subject areas. For these reasons, vertical scales may be less useful than VMS in helping educators close achievement gaps and move their students into their state-defined proficient category.

Prediction of category classification is a more useful interpretation of test scores in an AYP environment than an interpretation of student growth. A student may show growth in a single year, yet that growth rate may not be fast enough to move that student into the proficient or above category in the next year. Predicting which students in the subsequent year are likely to score in the proficient or above category may better assist schools in determining which students need supplemental instruction as schools make instructional plans on a school and student level based on test data.

Although category predictions are useful to educators, such predictions are also subject to error, and false positive and false negative classifications will occur. For example, a student may be predicted to be in the proficient category in a subsequent year, yet in that second year, he or she may not actually be classified in that category because the student was incorrectly classified as proficient in the first year. Because the AYP provisions of the NCLB (2001) require increasing percentages of students in the proficient category each year (or every 3 years, depending upon whether the state chose a linear or stair-step growth model), states may need to develop models to assist them in better determining which students may be borderline cases that impact AYP ratings within schools (Lissitz & Huynh, 2003).

SUMMARY AND DISCUSSION

Developmental (vertical) scales are often constructed for subject areas such as reading and mathematics, which are taught continuously in elementary schools, for example. In other subject areas that are grade specific, such as science and social studies at middle and high schools, such scales may not be justifiable and might be hard to construct. For tracking student progress for instruction and school accountability (including the NCLB Act [2001]) purposes, it may be more meaningful to rely on a system of VMS.

With national prominence, no doubt the NAEP has served as guiding light for many large-scale state assessment programs. In this article, we reviewed the steps the NAEP took in regard to the decision to decrease reliance on across-grade (vertical) scaling in a number of subject areas. We also described the two major conditions of a system of VMS and the assumptions under which such standards are justifiable and interpretable. The first condition pertains to a common set of policy definitions for the AL for all grades. This was done in NAEP, and many state assessment programs have followed the NAEP practice. The second condition pertains to some level of consistency in the percentages of students in important (if not all) ALs. Such consistency may be determined by prior knowledge about how a student progresses across grade levels or simply by a policy decision made in the light of data that are external but relevant to the subject area under assessment. Perhaps the most challenging task in creating a VMS system is the decision on the type of consistency just mentioned. Such consistency may be accomplished through increasing or decreasing trends or other types of trends that are reasonable for the assessment data. Therefore, a VMS system cannot be constructed in the absence of prior knowledge about student development and a governing body that is mandated to make or impose the consistency of student percentages across levels.

No doubt should be made about the usefulness of a vertical scale when it can be constructed. In the absence of a vertical scale, a system of VMS can also be used to track student progress or growth across years. Even when a vertical scale is available, Lissitz and Huynh (2003) still argued that when the focus of assessment is on influencing classroom instruction and teachers' adaptation to student needs, changes in the specific scale scores on a vertical scale do not convey a meaningful or practical message. Rather, Lissitz and Huynh suggested that the focus should be on each student meeting the achievement categories at a level that adequately prepares student for successful achievement in the next grade.

Finally, in the context of the NCLB Act (2001) legislation, standards that become suddenly stringent in a particular grade level may affect the percentage of students at or above the proficient level and thus adversely impact ratings on AYP for schools and states. Therefore, broad and consistent policy definitions regarding student achievement across years are essential, as is carefully deliberating the levels of achievement that are set for a testing program. A system of VMS would provide a common reporting system for all students while meeting the state school accountability requirements and the NCLB Act AYP requirements.

ACKNOWLEDGMENTS

We acknowledge the helpful comments and suggestions from Karen Barton, Mary Lyn Bourque, Steve Ferrara, Jeremy Finn, Susan Loomis, Canda Mueller, and Rebecca Zwick on earlier drafts of this article. We extend a note of gratitude to Gregory Cizek, Guest Editor, for his editorial comments and suggestions.

A version of this article was presented at the National Conference on Large-Scale Assessment, June 21, 2004, Boston, MA. An earlier version of this article was also presented at the invited symposium "Vertically Moderated Standards: Assumptions, Case Studies, and Applications to School Accountability and NCLB Adequate Yearly Progress" of the annual meeting of the National Council on Measurement in Education, April 2004, San Diego, CA.

REFERENCES

Bock, R. D. (1991, April). *Reporting problems created by the NAEP across-grade scales*. (Available from Huynh Huynh, College of Education, University of South Carolina, Columbia, SC 29208)

Buckendahl, C. W., Huynh, H., Siskind, T., & Saunders, J. (2005). A case study of vertically moderated standard setting for a state science assessment program. *Applied Measurement in Education, 18,* 83–98.

Colorado Department of Education (2003). *CSAP 2003 Technical Report–Part 2.* Retrieved August 9, 2004 from http://www.cde.state.co.us/cdeassess/ reports/2003/CSAP_Tech_part2.pdf

Cook, T.D., & Campbell, D.T. (1979). *Quasi-experimentation: Design and analysis issues for field settings.* Boston, MA: Houghton Mifflin.

CTB/McGraw-Hill. (1997). *TerraNova.* Monterey, CA: Authors.

CTB/McGraw-Hill. (2001). *TerraNova.* Monterey, CA: Authors.

Haertel, E. (1991). *Report on TRP analyses of issues concerning within-age versus cross-age scales for the National Assessment of Educational Progress.* Washington, DC: National Center for Education Statistics. (ERIC Document Reproduction Service No. 404367)

Harcourt Assessment, Inc. (2003). *Stanford English Language Proficiency Test technical manual.* San Antonio, TX: Author.

Harcourt Assessment, Inc. (2004). *Stanford Achievement Test series, Tenth Edition technical data report.* San Antonio, TX: Author.

Hieronymus, A. N., & Hoover, H. D. (1986). *Iowa Tests of Basic Skills manual for school administrators.* Chicago: Riverside.

Huynh, H., Barton, K., Meyer, P., Porchea, S., & Gallant, D. (2005). Consistency and predictive nature of vertically moderated standards for South Carolina's 1999 Palmetto Achievement Challenge Tests of English language arts and mathematics. *Journal of Applied Measurement in Education, 18,* 115–128.

Huynh, H., Meyer, P., & Barton, K. (2000). *Technical documentation for the South Carolina PACT-1999 tests.* Columbia: South Carolina Department of Education.

Illinois State Board of Education. (2003, October). *Social science assessment* framework (Grades 5 and 8). Retrieved July 22, 2004 from http://www.isbe.et/assessment/IAFSocialScience.rtf

Linn, R. L., & Baker, E. L. (1993, Winter). Comparing results from disparate assessments. In *The CRESST line.* Los Angeles: National Center for Research on Evaluation, Standards, & Student Testing.

Lissitz, R. W., & Huynh, H. (2003). Vertical equating for state assessments: Issues and solutions in determination of adequate yearly progress and school accountability. *Practical Assessment, Research & Evaluation, 8*(10). Retrieved October 7, 2003, from http://PAREonline.net/getvn.asp?v=8&n=10

Loomis, S. C., & Bourque, M. L. (2001a). From tradition to innovation: Standard setting on the National Assessment of Educational Progress. In G. J. Cizek (Ed.), *Setting performance standards: Concepts, methods, and perspectives* (175–217). Mahwah, NJ: Lawrence Erlbaum Associates, Inc.

Loomis, S. C., & Bourque, M. L. (Eds.). (2001b). *National Assessment of Educational Progress achievement levels, 1992–1998 for reading.* Washington, DC: National Assessment Governing Board.

Loomis, S. C., & Bourque, M. L. (Eds.). (2000c). *National Assessment of Educational Progress achievement levels, 1992–1998 for mathematics.* Washington, DC: National Assessment Governing Board.

Loomis, S. C., & Bourque, M. L. (Eds.). (2001d). *National Assessment of Educational Progress achievement levels, 1992–1998 for science.* Washington, DC: National Assessment Governing Board.

Mislevy, R. J. (1992). *Linking educational assessments: Concepts, issues, methods, and prospects.* Princeton, NJ: Educational Testing Service.

National Assessment Governing Board. (2002). *Reading framework for the 2003 National Assessment of Educational Progress.* Washington, DC: Author.

National Assessment Governing Board. (2003). Governing board awards contract to ACT to prepare 12th-grade math achievement levels. Retrieved May 10, 2004, from https://www.nagb.org

National Center for Education Statistics. (2004). *The nation's report card.* Retrieved June 1, 2004 from http://nces.ed.gov/nationsreportcard/

No Child Left Behind Act of 2001, Pub. L. No. 107-110, 115 Stat.1425 (2002).

Petersen, N. S., Kolen, M. J., & Hoover, H. D. (1989). Scaling, norming, and equating. In R.L. Linn, (Ed.) *Educational Measurement* (3rd ed., pp. 221–262). New York: American Council on Education and Macmillan Publishing Co.

Slinde, J. A., & Linn, R. L. (1977). Vertically equate tests: Fact or phantom? *Journal of Educational Measurement, 14,* 23–32.

South Carolina Code of Laws. (1998). *S.C. Education Accountability Act of 1998.* Retrieved February 2, 2004 from http://www.myscschools.com/archive/ednews/1998/98accact.htm

Tomkowicz, J., & Schaeffer, G. (2002, April). *Vertical scaling for custom criterion-referenced tests.* Paper presented at the annual meeting of the National Council on Measurement in Education, New Orleans, LA.

APPLIED MEASUREMENT IN EDUCATION, *18*(1), 115–128

Consistency and Predictive Nature of Vertically Moderated Standards for South Carolina's 1999 Palmetto Achievement Challenge Tests of Language Arts and Mathematics

Huynh Huynh
College of Education
University of South Carolina

Karen E. Barton
CTB/McGraw-Hill
Monterey, California

J. Patrick Meyer
Center for Assessment and Research Studies
James Madison University

Sameano Porchea and Dorinda Gallant
College of Education
University of South Carolina

This article reports on the consistency of the achievement-level classifications (*below basic, basic, proficient,* and *advanced*) established in 1999 for the South Carolina Palmetto Achievement Challenge Tests (PACT; Huynh, Meyer, & Barton, 2000) of English language arts and mathematics. It also utilizes the PACT longitudinal data files of student records from 2000 to 2002 to assess the predictive nature of these classifications. It was found that the proportion of students who obtained a basic or higher level classification, which is considered passing, on the same subject at the next grade level was about 80% for students at the basic category and at 99% for

Requests for reprints should be sent to Huynh Huynh, College of Education, University of South Carolina, Columbia, SC 29208. E-mail: huynh-huynh@sc.edu

the combined proficient and advanced category. For school accountability purposes, the original below basic category was split into a low category, *below basic-1*, and a high category, *below basic-2*. The passing proportion was 17% for below basic-1 students and about 43% for below basic-2 students. It was concluded that the PACT 1999 achievement categories fulfilled the function of identifying and characterizing students prepared for work at the next grade level as formulated in the policy definitions for these categories.

In 1998, South Carolina implemented the South Carolina Education Accountability Act (SCEAA; South Carolina Code of Laws, 1998). According to the act, "Accountability is defined as acceptance of the responsibility for improving student performance and taking actions to improve classroom performance by: the Governor, General Assembly, State Department of Education, colleges/universities, local boards, administrators, teachers, parents, students, (and) communities" (South Carolina Code of Laws, 1998). Among other things, the act requires that all subject areas, including mathematics, English language arts (ELA), science, and social studies, have specific content and performance standards for all grades.

To assess compliance with the requirements of the SCEAA (South Carolina Code of Laws, 1998) schools and districts are reviewed annually on the basis of their performance for the current year and their improvement from the previous year. The rating categories are *excellent, good, average, below average,* and *unsatisfactory.* These ratings are public information. They are posted in local and statewide newspapers in addition to being mailed to the schools and districts. Schools that do extremely well or show strong improvement receive the Palmetto Gold and Silver Awards, which include a monetary award depending on the availability of funds. Award criteria were developed by the South Carolina Education Oversight Committee (South Carolina Department of Education [SCDE], 2003), and any school performing above unsatisfactory in current rating or level of improvement across years is eligible. Poorly performing schools are required to develop performance improvement plans. These improvement plans must be reported to the press after they have been approved and revised by the state department of education and the State Board of Education. Schools and districts failing to improve after the implementation of the new performance improvement plan may be declared to be in a "state of emergency" by the State Board of Education and taken over by the state department of education. A state of emergency may also be declared if a school or district fails to implement the new performance improvement plan. A review team is required to report to the State Board of Education on the school's or district's performance, annually, for a period of 4 years.

SCEAA (South Carolina Code of Laws, 1998) rewards and consequences also apply to district and school personnel, teachers and students. One such consequence for a student is the implementation of an academic assistance plan. Teachers are required to design an academic assistance plan for students who do not achieve scores in at least the below basic-2 academic proficiency category, described later. By law, students who earn scores in the below basic-2 category for two consecutive years are subject to retention. In an effort to improve achievement, teacher specialists and principal mentors are installed at schools or districts that score poorly. In severe cases, principals may be replaced and removed from a school.

The federal No Child Left Behind (NCLB) Act of 2001 also addresses accountability issues, and, in particular, assessment issues across all grade levels (Kindergarten through Grade 12 [K–12]) and content areas. The NCLB Act contains four basic underlying principles: (a) stronger accountability for results, (b) increased flexibility and local control, (c) expanded options for parents, and (d) emphasis on teaching methods (U.S. Department of Education, n.d.). The NCLB Act requires adequate yearly progress reports for all schools based on the percentage of students scoring at the *proficient* level or higher on the statewide exams.

In response to both the state and federal accountability legislation, South Carolina developed the Palmetto Achievement Challenge Test (PACT; Huynh, Meyer, & Barton, 2000) for Grades 3 through 8 and the High School Assessment Program (HSAP) for Grades 9 through 12.

HISTORY AND DESCRIPTION
OF THE PACT ASSESSMENTS

We discuss a brief history of the PACT Assessments, including the political impetus and the standards that support the PACT, next. We describe the types of items and associating point values followed by a short exposition of the development of curriculum standards.

Overview

The catalysts for the development of the PACT were national trends in education that date back to the 1980s. Title I made challenging standards mandatory for states, whereas the 1983 report, *A Nation at Risk: The Imperative for Educational Reform*, by the National Commission on Excellence in Education, sought to do away with minimum competency evaluations and curricula. In light of these trends, the SCDE first considered revising the existing statewide tests —those comprising the Basic Skills Assessment Program (BSAP)—but then decided to create a new assessment program altogether. Additional factors that played a role in initiating the development of PACT included the age of BSAP, state legislation requiring new test items to be written, the desire to assess higher-level cognitive skills rather than minimum competency skills, and the desire to incorporate performance assessment items.

Item Types

Multiple-choice, open-response, open-ended, and extended-response items were used in the 1999 PACT. However, extended-response items were used only on ELA forms. Multiple-choice items required students to select an answer from several alternatives and were scored as either right or wrong. Open-response items obligated a student to respond with a few words or a sentence and were also scored as right or wrong. Open-ended items called for a more elaborate response and were scored using rubrics written specifically for each item. Most open-ended items were scored on a scale from 0 to 2 points or from 0 to 3 points, but a few were scored on a scale from 0 to 4. Finally, extended-response items required a lengthy response from students that was scored on a 15-point rubric (Huynh, Meyer, & Barton, 2000, pp. 27–28).

Curriculum Standards

A significant feature of the PACT is that South Carolina teachers are the primary authors both of the curriculum standards on which the PACT is based and the test blueprints (SCDE, 1998b, 1998c) that were written to give teachers specific information about the PACT. In 1993, to guide statewide education policy, the State Board of Education adopted the curriculum frameworks for foreign languages, mathematics, and the visual and performing arts. Frameworks for science, ELA, social studies, and physical education were completed and adopted in February 1996. The frameworks organized the core curriculum of each content area for each grade into content strands. Broad in scope, the content strands applied concepts and principles across the grade levels, from K–12. Content strands were accompanied by standards to indicate curriculum goals, to encourage change within the classroom, and to ensure quality. Teaching methodology, instructional materials, principles of assessment, support systems, and professional development issues were also discussed in the frameworks publications.

Four different committees were established to review and revise the frameworks. Suggestions for changes from teachers, administrators, parents, college educators, and business and community members within the state contributed to the refinement of the standards. These changes were approved by the State Board of Education in 1995 and 1996 and are outlined in the *South Carolina Mathematics Academic Achievement Standards* (SCDE, 1995) and the *South Carolina English Language Arts Academic Achievement Standards* (SCDE, 1996). These standards are also known as the "Gateway Standards." Each of these documents present content and process strands by grade-level groupings of primary (Kindergarten through Grade 3), elementary (Grades 4–6), middle school (Grades 7 and 8), and high school (Grades 9–12). The standards for each grade-level group indicate what students should know and be able to do by the end of Grades 3, 6, 8, and 12. Grades

3, 6, and 8 serve as benchmark years when performance is measured to determine each student's progress toward achieving the standards by the end of Grade 12.

District and school personnel and the public were asked to review the Gateway Standards and provide feedback to the State Board of Education. Changes from this review process were incorporated into a draft document written by the Governor's Performance Accountability Standards for Schools Commission for consideration by the State Board of Education. The draft documents submitted to the board in November 1997 listed specific objectives by content strand for each level from K–12. The grade-by-grade standards utilized the content objectives from the state of Virginia's Standards of Learning.

In the effort to emphasize the connections across grade levels, the grade-by-grade standards and the academic achievement standards were then combined, reorganized, and reformatted to create *Reading/English Language Arts: South Carolina Curriculum Standards* (SCDE, 1998d) and *Mathematics: South Carolina Curriculum Standards* (SCDE, 1998a). These documents provide user-friendly technical assistance guides for teachers and schools to help students meet a rigorous set of academic standards. Terminology consistent with Bloom's (1956) taxonomy of cognitive skills is used throughout these documents to indicate the cognitive level at which subject matter is to be taught. The documents also provide a complete picture of the specific knowledge and skills expected of students at each grade level. The PACT state-level assessment, instructional materials, and professional development activities are based on the standards in these documents.

Alignment With Other Standards

Efforts were made to align the PACT with the national standards of the National Assessment of Educational Progress (NAEP), the National Council of Teachers of Mathematics (NCTM), the National Council of Teachers of English (NCTE), and the Third International Mathematics and Science Standards (TIMSS). The alignment was implemented in three major steps. First, standards and frameworks committees that wrote the South Carolina curriculum standards were provided relevant content information about the NAEP, the NCTM, the NCTE, and the TIMSS. Second, the Council of Chief State School Officers reviewed the proposed standards to ensure that national standards were included. Last, PACT item writers were provided with samples from the NAEP and the TIMSS to serve as guidelines and examples.

Setting Performance Standards for Pact 1999

In this section, we describe the process by which the achievement-level classifications were developed. It includes the decision-making process for selecting a method for setting the classifications, the application of vertically moderated standards (VMSs), policy definitions of each achievement-level classification, and a description of the chosen bookmark method.

General Considerations

The 1999 PACT student data were reported using a within-grade scale system. For each grade and content area, the scale scores were set to have a mean that is 100 times the grade (i.e., Grade 3 mean is 300, Grade 4 mean is 400, etc.) and an *SD* of 16. Using these scales, comparisons can be made only for each content area and within each grade. The nature of the 1999 PACT data does not permit scale score comparison across grades.

In recent years, the National Assessment Governing Board has reported NAEP data using achievement levels (Bourque, 1997). In order to make comparisons across grades and follow the recommendations of the 1999 PACT Technical Advisory Committee (TAC), the SCDE defined four performance levels to describe student achievement on the 1999 PACT assessments for Grades 3 through 8: *below basic, basic, proficient*, and *advanced*.

After considering a variety of methods that were available for setting three cut scores to define these four achievement levels, the TAC narrowed the discussion to the modified Angoff (1971) and bookmark (Lewis, Mitzel, & Green, 1996) methods. The modified Angoff procedure was used in 1983 to set passing standards for reading and mathematics on the South Carolina BSAP 11th-grade tests (Huynh, 1985) and in 1986 for the South Carolina High School Exit Examinations (Huynh, Gleaton, & Seaman, 1990). The TAC recommended the bookmark method for establishing achievement levels for the 1999 PACT tests for Grades 3 and 8, and recommended interpolating cut scores for the intervening grades. A response probability of 67% (Huynh, 1994, 1998) was used.

VMSs

In retrospect, the standard-setting process recommended by the TAC for the 1999 PACT provided a system of vertically moderated standards as described by Huynh and Schneider (2004). As formulated by Huynh and Schneider, there are two basic elements in a system of VMSs. First, a set of common policy definitions (or achievement-level descriptors) of the achievement categories is used for all grades. Next, the percentage of students in important achievement categories is evaluated and a consistent trend line imposed to reflect prior knowledge about student growth and/or relevant external student achievement data. For example, after taking into account a multitude of factors, the National Assessment Governing Board of the NAEP decided on a set of cut scores for Grade 4 though Grade 12 that resulted in a decreasing percentage of students at the lowest category for reading and mathematics and in an increasing percentage for science (Huynh & Schneider, 2004).

Policy Definitions

Inherent in any standard-setting process is a general (or policy) definition of each achievement level. Policy definitions serve as guidelines for participants to follow in making decisions about the cut scores and are typically presented to the participants before the standard-setting takes place. The policy definitions for the four performance levels for PACT assessments are:

> *Below Basic*: A student who performs at the *Below Basic* level on the PACT has not met minimum expectations for student performance based on the curriculum standards approved by the State Board of Education. The student is not prepared for work at the next grade level.
>
> *Basic*: A student who performs at the *Basic* level on the PACT has met minimum expectations for student performance based on the curriculum standards approved by the State Board of Education. The student is minimally prepared for work at the next grade level. Performance at the *Basic* level means that the student has passed the test.
>
> *Proficient*: A student who performs at the *Proficient* level on the PACT has met expectations for student performance based on the curriculum standards approved by the State Board of Education. The student is well prepared for work at the next grade level. The *Proficient* level is the long-term goal for student performance in South Carolina.
>
> *Advanced*: A student who performs at the *Advanced* level on the PACT has exceeded expectations for student performance based on the curriculum standards approved by the State Board of Education. The student is very well prepared for work at the next grade level.

Implementation

The SCDE contracted with a testing company (CTB/McGraw-Hill) to use the bookmark process in setting performance levels on the 1999 PACT. The testing contractor prepared ordered-item booklets for the ELA and mathematics tests of Grades 3 and 8. Items in each booklet were assembled from easiest to most difficult, based on 1999 PACT student performance data. In the initial phases of the bookmarking process, participants became familiar with the tests by actually taking them. Then, in three rounds of judgments conducted over a two-day period, participants placed bookmarks at the three cut points: (a) differentiating between basic and below basic, (b) differentiating between proficient and basic, and (c) differentiating between advanced and proficient.

The first round of judgments included only individual decisions. The second round of judgments included small-group decisions and discussions of differences in the bookmarks set between groups. After the second round of bookmarking, a large group discussion was held before bookmarks were set in the third round. More details and results of the preceding bookmarking may be found in *The South Carolina Palmetto Achievement Challenge Tests: Grades 3 and 8 English Language Arts and Mathematics Bookmark Standard Setting Technical Report* (CTB/McGraw-Hill, 2000).

Following the standard-setting meetings, the testing contractor, under the direction of the SCDE, provided relevant information to the PACT TAC for review and deliberation. On TAC recommendation, the SCDE adopted the final cut scores for Grades 3 and 8 in ELA and mathematics tests. With minor refinement regarding rounding, the testing contractor used linear interpolation for the proportion of students in each of the four achievement categories to arrive at the cut scores for Grades 4 though 7 (D. Chayer, personal communication, June 28, 2004). In general, linear interpolation involves minor refinements of cut scores to even out or smooth the progression of cut scores up the vertical scale and to reflect similar proportions in each category across grades.

Table 1 provides the frequencies and percentages of students in the four achievement categories for each grade and test comprising the 1999 PACT.

TABLE 1
Percentage of Students in Each Performance Level by Grade
and Subject for the 1999 PACT

Grade	Content	N	Percentage in Each Performance Level			
			Below Basic	*Basic*	*Proficient*	*Advanced*
3	ELA	47,406	34.9	37.1	26.1	1.9
	Math	47,608	43.7	38.4	12.6	5.3
4	ELA	51,746	34.6	36.9	26.0	2.5
	Math	52,023	45.4	37.3	12.6	4.6
5	ELA	50,000	35.0	38.9	23.6	2.5
	Math	50,283	46.7	37.1	11.9	4.4
6	ELA	49,999	37.1	39.0	21.0	3.0
	Math	49,993	47.2	36.9	11.5	4.5
7	ELA	50,537	37.2	39.2	20.5	3.1
	Math	50,445	48.4	36.0	11.0	4.6
8	ELA	49,086	37.5	40.8	18.5	3.1
	Math	48,897	48.6	36.4	10.2	4.8

Note. PACT = South Carolina Palmetto Achievement Challenge Tests. ELA = English language arts. From *Technical Documentation for the 1999 Palmetto Achievement Tests of English Language Arts and Mathematics Grades Three Through Eight* (p.40), by H. Huynh, P. Meyer, and K. Barton, 2000. Columbia: South Carolina Department of Education.

CONSISTENCY OF ACHIEVEMENT-LEVEL CLASSIFICATIONS

It is important to evaluate the consistency (reliability) of student achievement-level classification into in order to use the PACT as an accountability measure. The *Standards for Educational and Psychological Testing* (American Educational Research Association, American Psychological Association, & National Council on Measurement in Education, 1999) explicitly states:

> When a test or combination of measures is used to make categorical decisions, estimates should be provided of the percentage of examinees who would be classified in the same way on two applications of the procedure, using the same form or alternate forms of the instrument. (Standard 2.15, p. 35)

In the context of classification, consistency (i.e., reliability) is similar to the traditional concept of test–retest or equivalent forms reliability. Classification consistency refers to the degree with which the achievement level for each student can be replicated upon retesting using the same form or an equivalent form (Huynh, 1976). As with most large-scale testing programs, repeated testing with the same form or an equivalent form is not always feasible. Therefore, a statistical model must be imposed on the data in order to estimate the consistency of achievement-level classifications. Although a number of procedures are available for this task, the beta-binomial model (Huynh, 1976) was used for the current estimation because of its ability to provide standard errors for the consistency estimates. The computation was performed using a FORTRAN computer program written by the first author (Huynh, 1979). (The computer program is available from Huynh Huynh on request.) Using the maximum possible score, mean, standard deviation, and Kuder–Richardson formula (KR21), the two parameters of the beta-binomial distribution are computed. Using the formulae in Huynh (1976), the program then projects the univariate and bivariate frequency distributions. It then computes the agreement and kappa indexes for the classification of students into achievement levels. The agreement index estimates the proportion of students who would be consistently classified into the same achievement levels on two equivalent administrations of the test. The kappa index, on the other hand, reflects the level of improvement beyond the chance level in the consistency of classifications.

Agreement indexes were computed for each grade and test for the case of four achievement levels, based on data from PACT 1999. Because PACT data are also used to identify below basic students who may need instructional assistance, computations were carried out using only two achievement-level categories: below basic and basic and above. For statistical completeness, the kappa indexes were also computed. Results of these consistency estimations are shown in Table 2. The data

TABLE 2
Consistency Indexes for 1999 PACT Achievement Levels

Grade	Content	Two Achievement Levels[a]		Four Achievement Levels	
		Agreement	κ	Agreement	κ
3	ELA	.859	.704	.685	.543
	Math	.862	.715	.735	.585
4	ELA	.877	.735	.727	.596
	Math	.841	.667	.709	.540
5	ELA	.972	.725	.713	.579
	Math	.853	.694	.731	.572
6	ELA	.877	.738	.747	.621
	Math	.859	.711	.745	.595
7	ELA	.882	.755	.749	.626
	Math	.843	.682	.715	.550
8	ELA	.893	.778	.775	.660
	Math	.883	.762	.799	.671

Note.   PACT = South Carolina Palmetto Achievement Challenge Tests. ELA = English language arts. From *Technical Documentation for the 1999 Palmetto Achievement Tests of English Language Arts and Mathematics Grades Three Through Eight* (p.48), by H. Huynh, P. Meyer, and K. Barton, 2000, Columbia: South Carolina Department of Education.
[a]The two achievement levels are *below basic* and *basic and above*.

show that the consistency indexes (agreement and kappa) for the four achievement levels are lower than those based on two categories. This is not surprising because classification using four levels would allow more opportunity to change the achievement levels. Hence, there would be more classification errors in the four achievement levels, resulting in lower consistency indexes.

We are not aware of an acceptable lower bound for various consistency indexes. Phillips (2000) cited a Texas court case in which a traditional test reliability index (such as alpha) of 0.85 was considered reasonable. At the below basic proportion of 40%, as found with the PACT 1999 tests, the bivariate normal table (Huynh, 1976; also reproduced in Crocker & Algina, 1986, p. 209) indicated that the test reliability index of 0.85 yields an agreement index of 0.82 for binary classifications. All agreement indexes for binary classifications (below basic vs. basic and above) of Table 2 exceed the lower limit of 0.82.

PREDICTIVE NATURE OF THE ACHIEVEMENT LEVELS

The PACT 1999 policy definitions cited previously specify that a student at the below basic level is not prepared for work at the next grade level, whereas a student who performs at the basic level is minimally prepared for work at the next grade level. The policy definitions also state that "performance at the Basic level means that the student has passed the test" (see, e.g., Huynh, Meyer, & Barton, 2000, p. 38). Thus, as a statement of policy, the achievement levels of basic, proficient, and advanced are treated as "passing categories," and passing students are prepared for subsequent work. As a consequence, given appropriate instruction, most passing students at one grade should be expected to pass the test at the next grade level. Also as a corollary, even when instruction is appropriate, it is likely a below basic or "nonpassing" student will not have a good chance of passing at the next grade. The main purpose of this section of the article is to document this conjecture regarding the predictive nature of the 1999 PACT achievement categories.

Two facts need to be presented. First, the 1999 PACT resulted in more than one third of students classified into the below basic category for each grade and subject. Consequently, the South Carolina Education Oversight Committee decided to split this category into two subcategories called *below basic-low* (BB–1) and *below basic-high* (BB–2) for the purpose of calculating school ratings. Next, a preliminary tabulation indicated that practically all advanced students passed the next grade level. Only a small number of students are at the advanced level. For convenience, the two highest categories proficient and advanced were collapsed into one category named *proficient and above* (P&A) in all subsequent analyses.

To explore the predictive ability of the classification of the PACT 1999 achievement levels, a 3-year longitudinal data set of matched student records was obtained from the SCDE Office of Assessment and the South Carolina Education Oversight Committee. For each student in the data file, PACT scores in ELA and mathematics as well as the achievement levels from the spring testing in 2000, 2001, and 2002 were available. The data were edited to exclude as many students that were tested off level as possible.

Table 3 shows the percentage of students in each current-grade achievement level who obtained a proficient or advanced level at the next grade level. The data files contain students in the current grades of third through sixth who were tested in Spring 2000. Data for students in the current grade of seventh are from seventh graders tested in Spring 2001.

The data in Table 3 indicate that the proportion of students who obtained a proficient or advanced level for the same subject at the next grade level is about 80% for students at the basic category and 99% for the combined P&A category. The data of Table 3 show that the proportion of students obtaining higher than basic is only 17% for BB–1 students and about 43% for BB–2 students. Thus, it may be said that the 1999 PACT achievement categories fulfill the function of classifying students as prepared to do work, and subsequently pass the test at the next grade level, as formulated in the policy definitions.

TABLE 3
Percentage of Students Passing the Next Grade

Subject Area	Grade	Testing Year	Percentage Passing at Next Grade			
			BB–1	BB–2	Basic	P&A
ELA	3	2000	31.5	59.1	86.8	99.2
	4	2000	18.7	45.2	80.3	98.8
	5	2000	13.1	37.1	80.1	99.3
	6	2000	17.5	47.4	82.9	99.1
	7	2001	13.7	42.1	82.6	99.5
Math	3	2000	22.9	44.9	76.5	97.6
	4	2000	11.6	36.0	77.1	98.8
	5	2000	14.6	44.9	84.2	99.6
	6	2000	11.5	34.3	74.4	98.5
	7	2001	15.1	40.5	78.9	99.2
All students			17.0	43.2	80.4	99.0

Note. BB–1 = *below basic-low*; BB–2 = *below basic-high*; P&A = *proficient and above*; ELA = English language arts.

DISCUSSION

The PACT provide a context to discuss VMSs. A standard-setting process conducted in 1999 yielded a set of VMSs for ELA and mathematics for Grades 3 through 8. Results support the consistency and predictive nature of the VMSs. The internal quality of the achievement levels was assessed via consistency (reliability) indexes. A focus was made on the agreement index or the proportion of students who would be classified in the same way by a hypothetical retesting. The agreement index for the two categories of below basic and basic and above ranged from 0.84 to 0.97 and exceeded the threshold considered reasonable in a Texas court case involving testing for high school certification.

A common set of policy definitions for the achievement levels was used for standard-setting at all grade levels. The definitions specify that at a student at the below basic level is not prepared for work at the next grade level, whereas a student who performs at the basic level is minimally prepared for work at the next grade level. As a consequence, most passing students at one grade should be expected to pass the test at the next grade level. Results indicated that over 80% of students in the basic category passed the same subject at the next grade level, whereas only 43% of the immediate preceding subcategory of below basic did. Thus, the data support the statements of student preparation at the next grade level that are found in the achievement category descriptions established for the 1999 PACT assessments.

In summary, the standards (i.e. cut scores) for the South Carolina 1999 PACT assessments were set through a vertically moderated process, from a retrospective view. The process relied on a rather "liberal" use of linear interpolation to arrive at the cut scores from the intermediate grades from the end-point grades. Even under this constraint, the resulting achievement classifications were found to display adequate internal consistency and predictive nature regarding students who were prepared for the materials to be taught in the next grade and who, therefore, would past the PACT test at this grade.

ACKNOWLEDGMENTS

We thank Theresa Siskind of the South Carolina Department of Education for her comments on an earlier draft of the article and for permission to use the PACT matched data files. Gratitude is extended to Garrett Mandeville for the tedious work in creating these files for the South Carolina Education Oversight Committee. We acknowledge the comments and suggestions of Canda Mueller, Steve Ferrara, and David Potter. We also extend a note of gratitude to Gregory Cizek, Guest Editor, for his editorial comments and suggestions.

REFERENCES

American Educational Research Association/American Psychological Association/National Council on Measurement in Education. (1999). *Standards for educational and psychological testing.* Washington, DC: Authors.

Angoff, W. H. (1971). Norms, scales, and equivalent scores. In R. L. Thorndike (Ed.). *Educational Measurement* (2nd ed., pp. 508–600). Washington, DC: American Council on Education.

Bloom, B. S. (Ed.). (1956). *Taxonomy of educational objectives: Handbook 1. The cognitive domain.* New York: McKay.

Bourque, M. L. (1997). Setting the NAEP Achievement Levels for the 1996 Mathematics Assessment. In *Technical Report of the NAEP 1996 State Assessment Program in Mathematics.* (Tech. Rep. Number NCES 97–951). Washington, DC: National Center for Education Statistics.

Crocker, L., & Algina, A. (1986). *Introduction to classical and modern test theory.* New York: Holt, Rinehart and Winston.

CTB/McGraw-Hill. (2000, February). *The South Carolina Palmetto Achievement Challenge Tests: Grades 3 and 8 English Language Arts and Mathematics Bookmark Standard Setting Technical Report.* Monterey, CA: Author.

Huynh, H. (1976). On the reliability of decisions in domain-referenced testing. *Journal of Educational Measurement, 13,* 253–264.

Huynh, H. (1979). Computational and statistical inference for two reliability indices based on the beta-binomial model. *Journal of Educational Statistics, 4,* 231–246.

Huynh, H. (1985). Assessing mastery of basic skills through summative testing. In D. U. Levine (Ed.), *Improving student achievement through mastery learning programs* (pp.185–201). San Francisco: Jossey-Bass.

Huynh, H. (1994, October). *Some technical aspects of standard-setting.* In *Proceedings of the Joint Conference on Standard Setting for Large-Scale Assessments of the National Assessment Governing*

Board (NAGB) and the National Center for Education Statistics (NCES; pp. 75–93). Washington, DC: NCES/NAGB.

Huynh, H. (1998). On score locations of binary and partial credit items and their applications to item mapping and criterion-referenced interpretation. *Journal of Educational and Behavioral Statistics, 23,* 35–56.

Huynh, H., Gleaton, J., & Seaman, S. P. (1992). *Technical documentation for the South Carolina High School Exit Examination of Reading and Mathematics* (2nd ed.). Columbia: University of South Carolina, College of Education.

Huynh, H., Meyer, P., & Barton, K. (1990). *Technical documentation for the 1999 Palmetto Achievement Tests of English language arts and mathematics grades three through eight.* Columbia: South Carolina Department of Education. Retrieved January 16, 2005, from http://www.myscschools.com

Huynh, H., & Schneider, M. C. (2004, April). *Vertically moderated standards as an alternative to vertical scaling: Assumptions, practices, and an odyssey through NAEP.* Paper presented at the annual meeting of the National Council on Measurement in Education, San Diego, CA.

Mitzel, H. C., Lewis, D. M., Patz, R. J., & Green, D. R. (2001). The bookmark procedure: Psychological perspectives. In G. J. Cizek (Ed.), Setting performance standards: Concepts, methods, and perspectives (pp. 249–281). Mahwah, NJ: Lawrence Erlbaum Associates, Inc.

National Commission on Excellence in Education (1983). *A nation at risk: The imperative for educational reform.* Washington D.C: Author.

No Child Left Behind Act of 2001, Pub. L. No. 107–110, 20 U.S.C. § 6311 (2002).

Phillips, S. E. (2000, April). Legal corner: GI forum v TEA. *NCME Newsletter, 8,* 2–3.

South Carolina Code of Laws. (1998). *S.C. Education Accountability Act of 1998,* Retrieved February 2, 2004 from http://www.myscschools.com/archive/ednews/1998/98accact.htm

South Carolina Department of Education. (1995). *South Carolina mathematics academic achievement standards.* Columbia: Author.

South Carolina Department of Education. (1996). *South Carolina English language arts academic achievement standards (Reading, writing, listening, speaking).* Columbia: Author.

South Carolina Department of Education. (1998a). *Mathematics: South Carolina curriculum standards.* Columbia: Author.

South Carolina Department of Education. (1998b). *PACT mathematics assessment: A blueprint for success.* Columbia:Author.

South Carolina Department of Education. (1998c). *PACT Reading/English language arts assessment: A blueprint for success.* Columbia: Author.

South Carolina Department of Education. (1998d). *Reading/English language arts: South Carolina curriculum standards.* Columbia: Author.

South Carolina Department of Education. (2003). *State honors more than 300 schools for outstanding academic performance.* Retrieved July 19, 2004, from http://www.myscschools.com/news/more.cfm?articleID=386

South Carolina Technical Advisory Committee. (1999, April 7–8).). Minutes. In *Minutes of the South Carolina Technical Advisory Committee meeting.* Columbia, SC.

U.S. Department of Education. (n.d.). *Introduction: No child left behind.* Retrieved February 2, 2004, from http://www.NoChildLeftBehind.gov/next/overview/index.html